CANCELLED CZECH FILES

ON THE RUN

Kate Pavelle

Mugen Press

Published by
Mugen Press
P.O. Box 11061
Pittsburgh, PA 15237, USA
www.mugenpress.com

This book is based on real events. Characters in this book have given the author permission to use their names and other identifying information. In rare cases, a name was changed to protect the innocent and the guilty alike.

Cancelled Czech Files: On the Run
Copyright © Kate Pavelle 2014
Cover art: Kate Pavelle and Miranda Pavelle

All rights reserved. No part of this book may be reproduced or transmitted in any form or by any means, electronic or mechanical, including photocopying, recording, or by any information storage and retrieval system without the written permission of the Publisher, except where permitted by law. To request permission and all other inquiries, contact Mugen Press, 110 Isolda Drive, Pittsburgh, PA 15209, USA.

ISBN: 978-1-62622-014-0

Printed in the United States of America
First Edition
January 31st, 2015

Praise for Kate Pavelle's Work

"… layered, detailed, emotionally fraught tale of wounded souls who discover that together they can find redemption and happiness."
~Joyfully Reviewed (*Wild Horses*)

"I loved the juxtaposition of Cayenne's wild nature with Kai's own temperament. They were both in need of a little taming."
~Reviews by Jessewave (*Wild Horses*)

"A murder mystery romance filled with suspense, adventure and obsessions."
~Gay List Book Reviews (*Zipper Fall*)

"… in *Breakfall* we keep getting hit with situation after situation that lead up to a cliffhanger that guarantees I will be getting my hands on book two as soon as it is available."
~Joyfully Jay (*Breakfall*)

"The ending has hope, sweetness, and the promise of another Sean and Asbjorn book that comes like a blow to the face. I can't wait."
~Cryselle's Bookshelf (*Breakfall*)

"Relativistic Phenomena is a sweet novella, and the tentative relationship between Tony and Ken is quite endearing."
~Scuttlebutt Reviews (*Relativistic Phenomena*)

Also by Kate Pavelle:

Novels

Wild Horses
Zipper Fall
Breakfall
Broken Gait

Shorts

Relativistic Phenomena
Attack of the Hedgehogs (Don't Try this at Home Anthology)
Wild Horses (Animal Magnetism Anthology)

Coming Soon:

In the Shadow of the Red Star (CCF)
Amerikan Dream (CCF)
Critical Timing (thriller)

Contents

Introduction · · · I
A bit of history behind my history

Chapter 1	The Crossing	1
Chapter 2	Taste of Freedom	9
Chapter 3	Strawberries	17
Chapter 4	Pennies From Heaven	25
Chapter 5	Smoke and Shadows	33
Chapter 6	The Careless Refugee Life	43
Chapter 7	Smooth Landing, Rough Surface	53
Chapter 8	In Vino Veritas	65
Chapter 9	To Pluck a Duck	81
Chapter 10	A Freshly Killed Fish	93
Chapter 11	Familial Closeness	107
Chapter 12	Meat Is So Basic	121
Chapter 13	K-Mart	125
Chapter 14	Boys Will Be Boys	135
Chapter 15	How Is the Dog?	143
Chapter 16	Only In America	149
Chapter 17	A Finely Honed Blade	159

A WORD OF THANKS

This book is dedicated to my parents, who took a giant leap of faith and took our family on this journey of adventure and discovery.

Our journey isn't unique. Whether you are experiencing it right now, having arrived from abroad recently, or whether your ancestors came to these shores generations ago, parts of you will likely identify with the events on these pages.

I'd like to thank all the people who helped us along the way. Our sponsors, Dana and Karel Kliment. My cousins' family, who followed us to America. All the kind neighbors, friends, and teachers who slowed down to give me the extra time I needed, shared household items, explained how things work here in America, and who encouraged us when the going got tough.

No book is complete without the input of the first readers and editors. Many people have commented upon, edited, and proofread these pages for me, and I thank them all. They are:

Kylah Dunn
Raichael McCarthy
P.D. Singer
Vladimir Stoy
Art and Barbara Pavelle
Scott Pavelle
Suzanna Pavelle

CANCELLED CZECH FILES
ON THE RUN

Kate Pavelle

INTRODUCTION

A bit of history behind my history

THE BOOK you are now holding represents years of adventure and introspection. Before I could write about it all, I had to learn enough English. I was born in the Czechoslovak Socialist Republic when the Beatles were new, longhaired rebels and the waves of their deceptively gentle music rippled through the air, altering the fabric of space-time as we know it.

WRITING this book has also taught me how much background information I take for granted in conversation, but have to explain for the benefit of many readers. Years and decades turn "yesterdays" into "historical information," and sometimes even "ancient myth."

I expect some of this background to be fairly esoteric for the post-Cold-War generations. Even people older than I am—those who lived through the Cold War here in the United States—may not be aware of how all the systemic poisons would twist peculiar aspects of family life under a totalitarian regime.

The American friends and family members patient enough to read my first efforts emphasized this. Yes, they'd heard something about this in general, but reading about actual events, and getting snippets of information as part of an actual life, that was fascinating, exotic, and sometimes even horrifying.

The communist State used people to spy on one another. Official search parties entered the homes of their fellow citizens several times a year, no warrant needed, in search of something illegal. Forbidden books, pornography, the radio set to anything but one of the official channels—all those were juicy finds for search groups known to us as the "Gray Plague." They asked the children about their parent's activities, presumably on the theory that children might guard their tongues less well.

I was well trained in how to answer and never slipped up.

My American boyfriend was horrified. "You mean they just walked in and searched your house?!"

I almost had to laugh. Of course they did. But no one really feared the agitators because you had to be an idiot to let them catch you. You knew they were coming. No, I explained, what really worried people were the spies in large apartment buildings because you might learn about two or three, but you knew there were always four or five.

Here, then, I'll make an attempt to acquaint you with some of the historical realities that wove through the fabric of my family's life back in the old country.

When I was two years old the Czechoslovak Communist Party embarked on a series of quasi-democratic reforms to clear away the corruption and allow True Socialist Ideals to thrive. For example, they didn't remove the censors from the state-owned newspapers, but they did allow those papers to expose problems—including corruption issues—that needed to be fixed. This reform effort is now known as the "Prague Spring."

WHEN I was three years old, the Soviet Union invaded Czechoslovakia in a powerful show of force. The reforms – especially that free press thing – had gone too far. They made the dictators in Kremlin nervous, because they would have been a bad precedent for other Eastern Bloc states, as well as for the common people living in the Soviet Union.

The Czech government was taken *en masse* for a "talking-to" in Moscow, while a tank battle raged over the control of the Prague TV broadcasting tower. Several bakers were shot in the street when they refused to give the Soviet soldiers their bread. It could have been worse, but it sure wasn't good.

By the time I was six, I'd learned there were two ways to speak: the things you could say at home, as long as you were quiet and the windows were closed, and the things you could say outside. When you were outside, and especially in school, you either remained silent or you lied. When asked, you professed your admiration for the Soviet Union and the Communist Party.

But only when asked.

Saying or doing the wrong thing wasn't a harmless mistake. Criticizing the regime meant you were a reactionary, and neither reactionaries nor their families would be admitted into high school or college. Merit mattered in the admissions process, but there was a strong political component as well. Dissent from the official party line could also cost a family member his or her job, or force a sibling into a career on a farm or in a factory.

My forked tongue distressed my father greatly. He believed that no child that age had any business being so well versed in the political double-speak of the time. It was one of the main reasons he chose to defect.

But the double-speak skills were necessary. Our family

already had one dissenter. My uncle was a political cartoonist who escaped to the West after the Prague Spring. Something about an ass-shaped cloud formation covering the city, with Soviet paratroopers falling right into it.

We were lucky that my grandmother balanced his politically incorrect existence. She was an actual member of the Communist Party and that offered a bit of protection. The irony was, she hadn't joined the Party voluntarily. A membership card had simply arrived in the mail one day. As a breadwinner at the time, she hadn't dared to send it back.

My grandfather had come from a wealthy family, and that made the government suspect him of elitist tendencies. In the end his anti-Nazi activity during the World War II proved strong enough to establish his patriotism, and the state eventually allowed him to work again, but in the meantime Grandma had been their only breadwinner. His family's property remained confiscated by the People, of course.

SHORTAGES of basic consumer goods filled my youth with fun scavenger hunts. The whole family stood in lines at multiple stores in an effort to purchase limited quantities of toilet paper, toothpaste, or meat. A centrally planned economy cannot possibly foresee the needs of the marketplace, and improvisation turned into beat-the-odds entertainment. Salt or baking soda on a toothbrush is an unappetizing yet effective method of cleaning teeth. Newspapers, torn into strips and rubbed until soft, can be a decent substitute for toilet paper. Government propaganda was thus elevated to a height of appreciation in the bathroom that it would have never reached while read over morning coffee.

Clothing bought from the stores was inevitably ugly

and low quality, so most households had at least one family member who would sew for the rest of the clan. My grandmother did the sewing for us with my mother's help. It was a rare woman who could walk into a fabric store without grand ambitions to create something the neighbors would think had been smuggled in from Paris. The West German "*Burda*" catalogue, which travelers smuggled from abroad, was a major source of the latest Western fashions and, more importantly, for sewing patterns.

Footwear was a bigger problem. You could make clothes, but not winter boots. Many people travelled to East Germany when they had to buy a new pair and then smuggled them in.

Czechoslovakia didn't want its citizens to get too entrepreneurial. If the customs officers caught you with a pair of East German boots, they would confiscate them. I grew up on stories of women who threw away their old, dilapidated shoes (depriving someone of a much needed hand-me-down), just so they could wear the new ones on their way back across the border. They even scuffed them a bit and got them nice and muddy, so they didn't look like a new purchase. Some of these women ended up walking home barefoot in the snow.

Customs officers could be capricious; after all, they had families too.

Anything Western was automatically in fashion. Blue jeans were a hard to come by status symbol typically owned by powerful people like dentists and plumbers. Sometimes one needed a plumber *now*, and being told "I'll be there in the next month or two if I can find an open slot," was hard to live with.

When that happened, prospective customers would have to ply the plumber with gifts to show their appreciation for his willingness to let them skip to the front of the line. Coffee, meat, and cigarettes were expected in the same way that tips are expected in a New York restaurant.

Alcohol was the bribe of choice when the scheduling really mattered. Blue jeans appeared when the problems got dire. A truly desperate victim of life's little insults might even scrounge up some Western currency.

Western currency, though illegal to either own or trade, was highly desirable because you could use it on any vacation. You could even bribe the roofer with it to come fix your leak right away. Roofers often had waiting lists five months long.

DESPITE ALL these hardships I had a lot of fun when I was a kid. Students advanced through elementary school as a group, with the same kids in every class year after year. We formed tight bonds of friendship, and even classroom enemies would close ranks against the adults in our lives, or the students in another section. The adults countered this by talking to one another much more than you see in modern America. If a kid misbehaved in school, a written note was reinforced by a telephone call. There was punishment both at school and at home.

Boys pulled their pants down after every grading period to show off the welts on their behinds. The adults still thought a good beating at home would reinforce the school's effort to educate.

Under those circumstances no kid would even dream of squealing on another. The pack instinct ran strong. We'd let one another copy homework, or even tests. The tricks of the trade trickled down through the years via classmates who had older brothers or sisters. We had a sense of solidarity and unity I haven't experienced since.

Our household in Prague had been the last in my class to buy a television, and one of the last ones to buy a car. We lived in a three-apartment family villa in Prague, with a garden large enough to provide a variety of fruit for canning and jamming for the winter.

There was a sense that the war, thirty years gone, could return and we would have nothing once again. There was a fear that our world could be upturned by a neighbor who reported us for improper political opinions, or for possession of forbidden books, or for listening to Western radio broadcasts.

The family knew people who spent time in jail as political prisoners. One of them was sentenced to forced labor in the uranium mines. There were also stories of abuse and torture in custody; dark whispers and insinuations that weren't voiced openly in front of the children. But the children had good ears, and were smart and perceptive enough to get the big picture. Beyond that we could let our imaginations run wild.

My family escaped when I was thirteen, spent several months in Munich, and then arrived in the United States about a year later. I was plunked in the middle of the ninth grade and was shocked to find that students were not separated during tests to prevent cheating. The teachers didn't even do a walk-through looking for cheat sheets. But I understood what it meant and adapted immediately. Personal integrity and honor were concepts I knew from old books. If they still mattered in an individualistic society I was happy to play along.

I found that a fellow student would have been offended —even appalled—if I offered to let her copy off my test. What, did I think they weren't good enough to get the right answers on their own? I thought it was sweet. Naïve and innocent, but admirable too.

One thing I didn't learn until later was that the pack behavior of my early years also served as the Czech sex education system. Parents didn't talk about such things at home and the schools had no such thing as a "health class". Kids were expected to learn from their older siblings, whisper the forbidden secrets to their best friends, who'd eventually trickle it down to the rest of the class. That's how the word spread to my classmates after I left. That was how my old friends learned about things like how babies are made, how to sneak out on a date, what constitutes a "French Kiss," how to use the new-style Western menstrual pads, and how to keep the old-fashioned sheets of fluffy cotton from leaking. I was separated from this support network just when those whispers began to appear, and therefore grew into womanhood in total ignorance of the facts of life.

MY FAMILY left Czechoslovakia on August 13th, 1979. This is the story of our adventurous journey and our fun-filled adjustment to the fascinating, exotic, and sometimes scary culture we now embrace.

Chapter 1

THE CROSSING

August 13th, 1979, Prague, Czechoslovakia

THEY MADE ME get out of bed at four-thirty in the morning. An ungodly time for a thirteen-year old.

Drowsy, I leaned my head against the back of my seat. Our powder blue Skoda sedan rumbled its way slowly through the winding cobblestone streets of Prague. A fat tongue of early morning fog snaked its way under the cliff that supported the castle and the battlements, engulfing the river and the ancient buildings on its banks.

We seemed to have been a little blue boat crossing a vast misty sea, the bridge under us a mere construct of my imagination. I turned toward my little brother Patrik in search of a more comfortable sleeping position.

"Katka, look! Hradčany! Well, look for crying out loud!" The urgency in my mother's voice roused me, so I lolled my head over for an obligatory peek.

Across the river, panoramic, loomed the famous Prague castle, seat of ancient Czech kings and modern usurpers. It looked unapproachable. Only the cliff and battlements jutted out into the breaking light of day.

"So what? I can see Hradčany any time."

"Don't be so sure," my mother said, her voice uncertain.

My father cleared his throat noisily, but the sound he made was almost obliterated by the vibrations of our wheels on the ancient stones. I turned back to my kid brother, who was squeezed in among the extra bags that wouldn't fit in the trunk. The car held everything an Eastern-bloc family of four might need for a two-week driving vacation to Austria, West Germany and Italy.

THE TRIP was a reward for my good grades, I'd been told. It would also do the family good to spend time together, they said. On a level which I barred from my full, waking consciousness I was aware of the arguments that were loud enough to hear, but not loud enough to understand through the solid brick walls. My brother and I had been spending a lot of time with our grandparents prior to this unexpected trip.

"Katerina, come upstairs and help me dry the dishes," my grandmother said in an effort to distract us from their discord. "Patrik, you come too. Grandpa will draw a locomotive for you."

The trip would be an exciting treat, and it would be so good to be together. I'd been thrilled when I was told, and I wished I was allowed to tell my friends.

"What you don't tell people won't be used against you later," my mother said. "It was hard enough just to get the visas. The less we attract attention to ourselves, the lesser a chance they'll be revoked."

No one left the Czechoslovak Socialist Republic without a visa. Visas to visit other countries of the Eastern Bloc were relatively common. Going West, having a chance to slip the leash—now that was a rare treat. Especially for a first trip abroad.

IT TOOK the better part of an hour to extricate ourselves from the grip of the antiquated city streets. Shortly after lunch we arrived closer to Austria. A couple of kilometers before the border, my father pulled the car onto a thin gravel strip by the two-lane asphalt road. He produced a rag and a spray-can of powder-blue paint, got out, and circled around to the front fender. He bent over to examine it.

My mother rolled down the window. "How does it look?"

"It's seeping that oily stuff again," he said. He wiped the fender clean with the rag, stepped back, and sprayed it with three judicious squirts of paint. Replacement front fenders for the Skoda-100 were hard to find. Our six-years old car was rusted through, and my father had spent the summer performing cosmetic surgery on it. With careful hands, he'd improvised and sculpted, until the left fender was symmetrical to the right and free of rusty holes. He reconstructed the shape, bonding the fragile metal to laminated fiberglass and the putty you use for bodywork.

"We'll wait here for awhile," he said. "I don't want the customs officials to smell fresh paint." Cars that looked too rusty could embarrass the State, and visa or no visa, might get you ordered to go back home.

The sun beat down on us, just standing there by the roadside. A rivulet of sweat fought its way from my scalp down my cheek and I wiped my face with my hand. Now my palm was hot and wet, and it tasted salty. Surreptitiously, I wiped my hand on my pants. Then I grabbed the handle and rolled my window down to cool off.

The warm smell of soil and vegetation mingled with the heady odor of drying paint, the road quiet. There wasn't much traffic going to Austria and back. The ditch by the right side of the car was overgrown with thistles and daisies. I heard the song of crickets and frogs.

"How are you kids doing back there?" my mother asked.

"Fine," I said. My brother and I sat still, the tension of our parents seeping through our beings, infecting us.

My father slid back behind the wheel. "Let's get our things in order. Documents?"

"Right here." My mother pulled out a thick yellow envelope and counted out the visas for each person. Her hands quivered briefly.

"Passports?"

"With the visas."

"Money?"

"Right here." She held up a much thinner envelope of government-allotted foreign currency.

My father turned to us kids. "Fix your hair," he said. "We want to make a good impression."

I combed my own and my brother's hair with our mother's comb.

"And fold that blanket neatly," my mother said. "The toys go back in the bag." Just as my father was reaching for the ignition, she glanced down at her hands, then turned to my father again, and said:

"I'm wearing too much jewelry."

Her fingers were encrusted with rings.

"Glove compartment?" my father asked, immediately changing his mind. "No, that's the first place they will search." The border-crossing searches were famous for their ruthless thoroughness.

My mother paused for a few heartbeats.

"I could have Katka wear some of it," she said. She turned around to look at my hands, and then asked with irritation, "Why did you have to bring those rings?"

I wore my two good rings. The bigger one was filigreed silver set with seven diminutive cabochons in a turquoise flower pattern. My father had given it to me for Christmas.

It was my first ever piece of real jewelry. No way was I undertaking a journey of this importance and magnitude, the first journey to the West, the first trip abroad, without proper jewelry! That would be like being hit by a bus while wearing dirty underwear.

The smaller ring was a find from a local swimming pool. The simple silver setting embraced a slightly cracked glass gem. I loved that ring. It was comfortable to wear, it fit me perfectly, and I liked to pretend it was platinum set with diamond.

"Here, give me those," she said. "The necklace too."

"Why?" I said.

"So I can give you my jewelry. Hurry up!"

"But I want to wear them!" I said, my voice an unabashed whine. I picked my very best things to wear in the West. If she brought too much, why was that my trouble? Why was that any trouble at all?

"Maybe she could keep the ring with the turquoises," my father said, trying to keep the peace. My mother was full of frantic energy, vibrating in the little passenger seat of our little car.

"Look. I know you like the necklace because it came from America, but see? Mine has a Kennedy dollar pendant." She gave me a conniving look. "He was an American president."

I hesitated.

"And it's real silver. Not just aluminum."

"Well, I guess that would be okay," I said. I handed my precious necklace over to my mother and put hers on.

"And hand over that piece of broken glass. You can wear this one. They look almost the same." Her voice was like a rose, beautiful and barbed with thorns.

This was an easier trade.

I knew this ring. It used to belong to her father. Its delicate platinum and white gold setting showed off a small diamond to great advantage, and I hoped it would be mine someday.

"Do I get to keep it?" I asked daringly.

"No!" She bristled. "You'll have to give it back. But you will have many other rings someday."

I pulled my special silver ring off with care and handed it over. She palmed it together with my necklace and threw it all out the open window into the overgrown ditch.

The sun beat down on the chirping crickets.

"How could you!" I screamed.

She held out her ring. "Now put this ring on," she said.

"No. I don't want it anymore." I dug my heels in. Her long, painted fingernails circled my wrist and thrust the ring into the palm of my hand and just for a fleeting moment I held the image of it flying out my own open window, its trajectory following its predecessors. My head bent, I stared at it in the palm of my hand, transfixed. My whole body hummed like an overtightened string as I struggled to stay my hand. The ring she pressed into my hand was a family heirloom. My heart screamed revenge, yet I just couldn't do it. As long as I kept my eyes on the thin, warm piece of metal in my hand, I knew I'd retain control. I didn't dare look away from it, afraid my arm would spring up like a catapult and release all that crimson, heated anger along with the ring.

Grandpa's ring.

My father drew a long, deep breath in the driver's seat, then let it out all at once.

"Was that really necessary?" he asked my mother.

"What would you have done?"

"It could have gotten tossed on the bottom of the trunk. Or on the floor."

"And if they found it?"

"An accident. You know how kids are."

There was a deep hum in my ears. I felt the stinging in my eyes, the tightness in my chest.

My mother looked at my flushed face. "Don't you dare cry," she snapped. "We're too close to the border."

"Your mother maybe shouldn't have done that," my father said in a measured voice. "Why don't you wear her special diamond ring, you know, to make up for what she did."

"If they ask you, tell them you got the ring from your grandmother," my mother said. "Tell them it's just silver."

I slipped the ring onto my finger. It fit me perfectly. I smiled. Maybe I could keep it, since she threw my other ring out the window.

We pulled into the nonexistent traffic. The hum of the small engine overpowered the serenading crickets and frogs. Soon I saw the border coming up from the back seat of the car. There was a guard shack and rails barring the way across the road, and thick vegetation which screened the structure of the border itself. I was sorely tempted to lift my head and see if could catch a glimpse of the famous fences guarded by dogs, or the fallow mine fields. I tried not to look.

With great earnestness I played with my brother.

We stayed very quiet.

The customs official checked our visas, our passports. He looked inside all the windows. Overcome by curiosity, I lifted my head just for a split-second. Our eyes met. He held my gaze for a heartbeat, then smiled at me and waved us on.

We were through.

Chapter 2

TASTE OF FREEDOM

August 13th, 1979, Austria

THE ROLLING hills of the Black Forest looked much the same on the Austrian side as they had back home. My parents wore big, victorious grins. I could see them breathing deeper.

"Let's not get happy too quick," my mother said. "Austria is loaded with Czech spies."

"We won't stay long," my father replied. "We'll drive straight through to Munich."

I looked out my window, absorbing the sun-drenched landscape of the first foreign country I had ever seen.

The smooth, winding road led us through deep, mixed forest of the border area. After several kilometers we began to see small vacation retreats. Their stone and wood construction looked similar to the ones we had seen in the mountains wreathing Bohemia. The wooden shutters were open for the summer, their window boxes overflowing with a profusion of color. The older mountain cottages were decorated in gingerbread house designs of wood nailed onto wood, painted with bright colors. Just like in Bohemia, except brighter somehow, as though their owners could afford fresh paint more often.

Further south, mountainous woods yielded to fertile plains. Soon we passed through a village. The pristine houses had the ubiquitous flower-boxes in the windows. The road was in good repair. It looked nothing like Czech villages, where the houses were gray with pollution, neglected and desolate. Only weeds thrived, pushing their way through the broken asphalt.

"Aren't we staying in Austria for awhile?" I asked, testing the waters. The talk of "just driving through" needed investigating.

"We'll see," my father said. "Just look around. See that gray mass ahead of us? That's the Alps. We'll go south a bit, then turn West."

TWO HOURS and many villages later, we entered a small town. The square was paved in old-fashioned cobblestones and surrounded by baroque buildings. Even the air seemed brighter. It could have been any small town in Bohemia, except in Technicolor.

We parked and got out of the car. We all needed a rest room. There was no need to buy refreshments, for my mother had prepared our provisions ahead of time. No Czechs but high party officials could afford to eat in Western restaurants, so we all brought food with us. The standard mainstays of Czech travel food were a thermos of tea so nobody got sick by drinking polluted well water, bread and butter, wiener schnitzels, hard-boiled eggs, and whatever fruit was ripe in the garden. Travel money was reserved for gas and lodging.

I gawked curiously as we made our way around the square, until a bright flash of color caught my eye.

"Look, Mom, strawberries!"

And there they were, on a sidewalk table in front of a greengrocer's shop with not a speck of field dirt on them.

They sat in tidy green paper baskets, gleaming and unguarded. Only a sign on a blackboard said, "3.50".

"You'd never see strawberries like that in Prague," my mother said, admiring them. "And look at those cute little baskets they come in!"

In Prague, strawberries arrived only once a year. They were bruised and dirty from the field, their juices seeping through the cheap paper bag, but they were a rare and fragrant delicacy.

"If you left a table of strawberries out like that in Prague, they'd be gone," my father said.

"You mean people would buy them right up?" I asked.

"No. I mean people would steal them." He gave me a grave and measured look. "We are in the West now. Some people might feel prejudiced against us so it's especially important to never steal. Some things that were tolerated at home, like snitching fruit from the neighbor's garden, would be considered a great embarrassment here. To us, as a family. And to us as Czechs, too."

"I know."

"I know you know." My father fished some money out of his pocket. "How about we buy a little basket?"

"They aren't cheap," my mother said, eyeing them wistfully.

They weren't cheap, but they were ripe, and clean, our first taste of the sweet West.

DARKNESS found us passing through a village by a large lake at the foot of the Alps. Only an hour ago we'd seen sailboats on it. They were no longer visible, the celestial light bulb suddenly extinguished in the proximity of the mountains.

"Look," my mother pointed to a sign on a private home. "*Zimmer frei*. A room for rent. Let's see if they have a vacancy."

A small Austrian woman showed us to our room, then led us to the bathroom next door. "*Das Dusch*", she said, pointing at the shower. She pointed at other things and said their name in German, too. Then she said something very slowly to my parents, and left.

It amused me to see how very Austrian the Austrians were. They defended their own space vigilantly, yet respected yours. They spoke quietly. Everything was orderly, clean, and in good repair. Their voices were hushed, not even resembling the loud, honking speech of German tourists typically seen in Czechoslovakia. They were more like the Czechs than like the Germans, I decided. Yet, at the same time they were not.

My father brought our suitcases inside while I craned my neck, examining the place where I would spend my first night in a foreign country. The room was a remodeled attic, large enough to sleep six people, and fragrant with wood paneling that covered the sloped ceiling. I looked around. It looked so new and fresh—all smooth wood and warmth and bright, clean fabrics.

My mother set out our dinner on a small, round table, unpacking our provender with deliberate care. We sat down to eat, passing the mustard and salt around. I chewed the solid, Czech rye bread with caraway seeds. It felt oddly comforting, being so far away, and yet eating the bread of my homeland.

I swallowed, and broke the silence. "Are we defecting?"

Time froze for everyone but my brother. He sat in a chair too high for his legs, kicking and eating a wiener schnitzel. My parents stopped in mid-motion, hands stilled in the midst of their customary dining motions.

The clock ticked on the wall, louder and louder, and then my father swallowed his mouthful and said, "Yes as a matter of fact, we are."

"Why didn't you tell me?" I asked, accusation in my voice. They'd left me out of the loop. Like a little kid.

"It was safer that way," my father said. "We thought you would want to say good-bye to your friends, and they might tell their parents, and then it wouldn't be a secret anymore. We'd go to jail."

I thought of my friends. Tamara, Iveta, Veronika. Tamara's father was an army officer, and half-Russian to boot.

"OK," I conceded. "But what about Grandma and Grandpa? And Karina? I could have at least said good-bye to Karina—she wouldn't have said anything." Karina was one quarter wolf and three-quarters German shepherd. The reality of her absence began to sink in, leaving an empty space in my chest.

"It's safer for them not to know."

DINNER was over. My brother Patrik was excused from the table to go play on the floor. My mother gathered the uneaten food and packed it for the next day. My father stood up and looked at us like a general surveying his troops, winning us over for his mission.

"It's time we discussed this situation. Maybe you are old enough," he nodded in my direction. My mother sat silent, her head bowed.

"We decided—your mother and I—that it's best for you kids to grow up in the West. You will have more opportunities. We'd like you to grow up so you don't have to watch what you say all the time, speaking your mind only at home and lying to everybody else. You'll be able to attend a high school instead of a vocational school, and even a university. Nobody will worry whether your parents are members of the Communist Party. In the West, being accepted into a school is based on your grades, not on politics, or on whether there are too many educated people in your family already. We'll get to vote in real elections. You won't have to lie about what you really think."

My father stood up, his voice raised in pitch somewhat as he began to pace.

"This will be hard at first. We are leaving everything behind. If we write home, our mail will be censored or confiscated. All telephone calls will be tapped."

I nodded. Everybody knew these things. Letters from Uncle Slavek—my mother's brother—came from England opened and read. He often wrote in a nonsensical code just to aggravate the censors, though in all likelihood it merely served to raise my grandmother's blood pressure.

"Now the question is, where do we want to settle?" my father asked, then ticked the choices off on his fingers.

"We could stay here in Austria," he said. "But it would be close to home."

"Austria is full of Czech spies," my mother interjected. "One of the kids could get kidnapped. They could force the whole family to return." Her eyes wandered over to my brother, who was drawing a train with the oblivious focus of a four-year old.

"Then there is Switzerland," my father said. "But it takes fifteen years to become a citizen."

"And the Swiss are so reserved," my mother said.

We all shook our heads. Nobody was really excited about Switzerland.

"Then there is South Africa," my father ticked of another finger. "But the political situation…"

"South Africa is a powder-keg," my mother said disdainfully.

"Why?" I asked. Political situations weren't part of the school's State-approved curriculum. My parents listened to Radio Free America and BBC Europe for real—albeit forbidden—news.

"All those blacks; not enough whites. Someday the blacks will rebel, and it will be a blood bath. We would be sorely outnumbered. And, do you really want to live in Africa? What of the weather? And what of the strange tropical diseases?"

The dire scenario of civil war and malaria overpowered any romantic notions about the mysterious Dark Continent.

"OK, no Africa," I said.

"Then there is Germany," my father said.

"That's also too close to home," my mother said. "Besides, you are always a foreigner in Germany."

"England isn't taking refugees right now, so that leaves America," my father said. "Or Australia, or New Zealand."

"We're not moving to Australia," my mother said with a finality that I found unfortunate. "It started out as a penal colony. And it's too far away."

So much for the banana plantations, and the kangaroos, and the endless, blue ocean. I let out a quiet sigh.

"America, then," my father said.

"America," we all nodded.

Yet even America was far, far away. America was a theoretical concept populated by mounted and armed cowboys, railroad-building prospectors, and Indian tribes. But there was freedom and wealth in America. In America, everyone was equal. You could say the President of the United States was a retarded idiot, and even if you said it in front of a police officer, you still wouldn't go to jail for it.

"Hooray, we are going to America!" I whooped. "I was going to escape to America when I finished school anyhow."

My mother looked at me with considerable surprise. My father's shock was immediately replaced by a wide smile of relief.

"To America, then!" he said, grinning.

"To America," my mother said.

My brother looked up from his drawing, looking from one person to another, trying to determine what the excitement was all about.

"We will go on an airplane, Patrik," my father told him. "A big airplane, all the way to America. Would you like us to draw an airplane?"

The energy of tension and excitement slowly drained out of the room. The incandescent light reflected off the blond wooden paneling on the walls. It felt warm and comfortable.

I went to sleep with a smile on my face that night, dreaming of America. I pictured myself adopted by an Apache tribe, living on a reservation and carrying a six-shooter on my hip. I knew I'd ride horses instead of driving cars. I would live like a noble savage. My family could stay out East. I would move away and live on an Indian reservation as soon as I was allowed. I was going to America, and in America I could do whatever I wanted. That thought was sweet, sweeter even than a whole bushel of Austrian strawberries.

Chapter 3

STRAWBERRIES

August 25^h, 1979, Munich, West Germany

WE LEFT the too-small room of Penzion Muller on the outskirts of Munich after only one week in favor of Penzion Beck. The main advantage of our new abode, aside from a much larger room, was its location by the Isaar River. Almost every day, we'd walk upstream and then hang a right toward the downtown area and the pedestrian zone.

The central location was a necessity ever since dad sold our brave little Czech car for twenty Deutschmarks to a used car dealer. This way we could walk everywhere—and walking was cheaper than having to pay for the Metro.

We were waiting for the right refugee paperwork, and the wheels of bureaucracy turned slowly even in Germany. Everything took time. With not much else to do, we walked several hours every day. I didn't mind the room at first. Pension Beck was a classy place. The old elevator was a lovely, iron-wrought cage which we weren't allowed to use, because our mother called it a "death trap."

The room had four beds, a kitchenette, and a table with four chairs. When rain foiled our plans to get out, I'd lie on my bed and trace the opulent, rococo designs of the expensive wallpaper with my eyes. And I'd never get bored that way, because the room had four different kinds of wallpaper in it, one on each wall. The colors and patterns were mesmerizing, and I was enchanted by their novelty.

As soon as the rain stopped, we'd escape the confines of the Penzion to discover the adventures of the West. Upstream and downstream, onto little island parks, into playgrounds for children, into museums and stores. We marveled at everything. Munich was clean, people were relaxed and pleasant, and merchandise was plentiful.

Money was tight, though. We had to make tough choices. My parents requested a German political asylum immediately, and when that bit of paperwork came through, they received enough money to pay for the penzion room and a food allowance. It wasn't a lot of money, yet to us it seemed a fortune.

The Marienplatz pedestrian zone was full of farmers, selling their seasonal produce. When I saw the prices of fruit in Munich, I realized how fortunate we had been back in Prague. Grandpa's three-apartment family villa, where we lived, had a generous garden planted by my great-grandfather. It yielded three varieties of pears, three varieties of apples, two plums, a sour cherry, apricots, currants and gooseberries. We were lucky compared to many of our treeless neighbors, and shared the extra fruit freely.

The grocery store in Prague carried only seasonal, boring vegetables: carrots and cauliflower, cabbage and onions. Potatoes were a staple ordered in bulk, delivered directly to the root cellar. The Prague apples available for sale looked sad and bruised compared to the ones straight off the tree. I was spoiled by the bounty our trees had offered. Now we had to not only buy all our fruit, we had to pay real West-German marks for it.

We saw multiple varieties of all kinds of fruit. Some were unknown to us. They had all the colors of the rainbow, fresh and clean. The grapes were large and fragrant, or small and delicate. The plums came in any size and color imaginable. And then, to top it off, one day a truck backed into the marketplace, straight from the strawberry fields.

A paper cone of strawberries cost 1.75 marks, and it would have made a fine dessert for a family of four. The four of us hungered for more than just food. We saw the bounty, the luxury, and the rich red color of strawberry juice seeping through the recycled paper of the cone. We ate nothing but strawberries that day.

They were fresh from the field, warmed by the sun, with an occasional speck of dirt on them. Leaning against a statue of a brass boar, I picked them out of the cone one by one, letting the sweet fruit melt in my mouth, allowing the aromatic flavor to transport me to another time and place.

MY GRANDMOTHER knew how much I loved strawberries, so she planted some. She wanted more than just that one seasonal opportunity at sweet, aromatic bliss. Strawberries were delivered to the state produce store only once a year, and the word would immediately spread. Mothers and grandmothers would take turns standing in a long line, patiently waiting their turn to buy their allotted one kilogram of the bruised, fragrant fruit. Only one kilogram per family—that way there would be enough for almost everyone.

So Grandma planted strawberries in our garden. They failed to thrive, a fact she blamed partly on the shade cast by the fruit trees, but also on my tendency to pick them as soon as they were barely pink.

"Now Katerina, I am going out and when I come back, I will count the strawberries again. There are eighteen of them now," my grandmother would say. I was her little bird, she was the scarecrow.

Our neighbor to the south, Mrs. Kloudova, had a much smaller yard and no trees at all. This yielded perfect strawberry-growing conditions. Mrs. Kloudova was a retired widow and spent considerable amount of time working the enormous strawberry patch right by our fence. Her strawberries were large and plentiful. When I stood by the chain-link fence just right, the summer breeze brought their fabulous fragrance straight to my nose.

"Grandma, could I ask Mrs. Kloudova for a few of her strawberries?"

"No! That would not be appropriate. We do not ask others for food. How would that look?"

Back then, my nine-year old little heart refused to do without. I wasn't allowed to ask. Surely there had to be another way.

I conceived my plan within a week and quickly put it into action. First I found a dowel long enough to reach the strawberry patch through the fence. Then I stripped insulation from a surplus piece of heavy copper wire. I shaped the thick wire into a crown-like, circular shape, and attached it to the dowel. After that, I found a piece of scrap fabric.

"What are you up to, Katerina?" my grandmother asked, ever vigilant.

"I am sewing a little bag," I replied truthfully, and she left, satisfied to see me occupied with such a feminine, age-appropriate task. As soon as she left, I attached the little bag to the circular crown with a copious amount of thread. Now my strawberry harvester was complete.

I waited until Sunday. On Sundays, every family in the neighborhood marched to the beat of the same drummer.

At high noon, not a minute later, the whole neighborhood sat down to their tables set with good china and ate a three-course hot lunch. The adults would linger over their coffee and dessert. The children would be excused.

That was my window of opportunity.

I ran down the four flights of stairs, then up into the garden. I looked around. The coast was clear, the neighboring yards were deserted because the neighbors, just like us, were lingering over their Sunday lunch. I casually walked up to the chain link fence and knelt behind a large dahlia plant. My bare knees pressed into the warm, turned soil as I leaned toward the fence.

I inserted the head of my strawberry harvester through the diamond-shaped opening in the chain link fence and aimed for the largest strawberry within reach. It took me three tries before I snagged it and manipulated it into the bag of my strawberry harvester. I tugged gently, over and over. The stem gave, and I could finally pull my prize to our side of the fence.

And here I learned the lesson of greed. The combined size of the strawberry harvester and the largest strawberry was too large to pass through the opening in the chain link fence! I turn my tool upside down, trying to catch the strawberry in my fingers and pull it through, but it tumbled out, brushed my fingertips on its way down, and landed in the sun-warmed soil. So near, and yet forever out of reach.

Wiser now, I went for a medium strawberry next. It fit through the fence just fine, and I carefully manipulated it to my side. It spilled into the palm of my hand, red and warm and luscious. I put it in my mouth and its flavor was so fine, so sweet, so unforgettable it shook me to the very core of my being.

I came to my senses and looked around. The coast was still clear. Nobody yelled, "Stop, thief!" out of their window. I continued, ignoring the cramping in my shoulders, the burning in my triceps. When I was pulling my fourth strawberry through the fence, a shadow fell over me.

"Katerina!" My grandmother hissed. "What are you doing! Suppose somebody saw you. What an embarrassment for the family!"

Then she looked at my strawberry harvester. Retired teacher's curiosity won out.

"Let me see that," she said. I spilled the fourth strawberry into my hand and surrendered my tool. She examined its construction.

"Did you make it yourself? This is simply amazing! All that effort for a few strawberries. Why didn't you just ask?" She looked at the strawberry in my hand. "You may as well eat that. There is no point in wasting good food."

Munich's strawberries were excellent, just like the ones in Austria, but I still remember the ill-gained fruit of my youth as the best of them all.

EVERY TWO or three days, we went food shopping. We had to go often, for we lacked a refrigerator in our penzion room. After the strawberry orgies of the previous week we spied a bright green, ovoid fruit.

"*Avokado*", the sign said. Its name spoke of exotic lands far beyond our reach. Surely no one in Prague had ever tried the mysterious avocado. But it was expensive, and so my mother and father wrestled with their great curiosity for a long time.

"Maybe this time we could try the avocado," they said over and over as we selected our fruit for the next three days. The avocado was worth six apples in price. If it was that expensive, surely it must be very good or else why would the merchants sell it?

One day the planets were aligned just so, and all four of us decided we were ready to give up ordinary fruit in favor of the fantastically bright-green avocado. My mother bought one single avocado and placed it in her canvas shopping bag with other groceries.

With great ceremony and deliberation, we settled down around the square formica table.

The avocado was in the middle of the table.

Next to it was a sharp knife.

Each one of us had a small plate awaiting our share.

My mother hefted the shiny fruit and carefully examined its geometry, deciding how to perform the first incision.

"It has a fairly tough skin," she reported. Her knife pared the skin carefully; it barely peeled off the pale green flesh within. My father leaned over curiously.

"I wonder what it tastes like," he said eagerly. We tasted so many great cheeses and sausages and fruit in Germany. It was sure to be good.

"The flesh is hard to cut," my mother admitted after a brief struggle. The avocado, devoid of skin, slipped about on her plate. She struggled a bit, then placed a thin slice of pale green flesh on everyone's plate.

We looked at one another. This was the moment we had been anticipating for weeks. As one, we all took a bite.

Sounds of spitting followed.

"It's slippery, like soap."

"It's bitter!"

"It has no taste."

"It's really hard to chew."

My father cut few more pieces off the avocado, removing enough substance to reach the treasure within.

"Look, we are eating the wrong part!" he crowed with great triumph. "The part you eat must be here, inside. What we were eating wasn't the flesh; it's just a part of the thick skin."

He removed the pale green mass, revealing a large, brown nut. He went at it with the knife, over and over, until he succeeded in splitting it in half. The brown skin of the nut revealed a pleasing, creamy flesh.

"I guess they eat this part," my father said. He offered everyone a small fragment of the nut. As one, we tasted it.

Sounds of spitting followed.

"This is even worse!"

"This is even more bitter!"

"So what do they eat, then?"

"Maybe it needs to be roasted, like a chestnut."

We surveyed the avocado carnage on the small formica table. We had bought this expensive fruit; obviously somebody found it of great value, but why? We embarked on a reevaluation exercise. We tasted every single component again, even the glossy green skin. Even the brown shell of the nut inside.

"This is the most disgusting fruit I have ever tasted," my mother said. We nodded hesitantly, not wanting to slander a fruit so expensive.

But not all was lost. We found the bitter taste in the mouth was easily chased away by a slice of real imported American Wonder Bread, topped with the famously delectable Nutella. The hazelnut and chocolate Nutella, spread onto the spongy whiteness of a real American Wonder Bread, tasted like birthday cake.

Chapter 4

PENNIES FROM HEAVEN

October 14ᵗʰ, 1979, Munich, West Germany

Munich in the fall was enchanting. The leaves were turning, and the weather was still warm enough to swim in the river. The natives even sunbathed naked, and the passersby on the city promenades paid them very little attention. Market stalls sprang up on Marienplatz, right between the Kaufhof department store and the ancient church with its magnificent astrological clock. So many stalls. So many stores. So much to buy, to see.

It was 1979 and I was thirteen. We walked through the shopping areas daily, and for purely recreational reasons. There was no reason or money to buy anything most of the time, but surveying the assortment of merchandise was entertainment enough. And there were no lines. No queues of mothers and fathers, stopping at a store during their lunch-break and seeing a line of people, joining it first and only then asking, "What are people waiting for? Is it toothpaste? Coffee? Or toilet paper? We haven't had toilet paper in weeks."

My mother cooked instant rice and fried a liver steak for us at least three times a week on the little electric burner of our pension room. It was the cheapest meat, but it was always available. At least once a week we had a rotisserie chicken. And there was produce from the market.

My brother Patrik was a four year old with "the power of cute". He would smile at the German merchant women and say, "*Grüss Gott*", a common Bavarian greeting. "God Bless." And they would smile at him, say "Grüss Gott" back and sometimes give him an apple, or a plum, or a pear. This was good—a free piece of fruit meant my mother could buy one less and save money.

This abundance of goods meant, naturally, that us kids wanted some loot. What good was it to be in West Germany, abandoning kin and kith and friends and family dog, and not even get any loot? There was an ice cream man, and there were little Matchbox cars, and my brother Patrik was interested in those.

My father, in his wisdom, decided that Patrik could learn to save for them. After all, we were in the West now, were we not? Even the children needed to manage money… somehow. So after every shopping trip, my four-year-old brother got the spare change.

At thirteen years of age, my yearnings leaned more towards bejeweled tortoise hair combs than toward Matchbox cars. The most elaborate one sat displayed among its lesser cousins in a store window, carved in intricate knotwork and set with brilliant jewels. It was the very picture of Western sophistication, and it cost thirty-two marks.

"Why don't I get spare change, too?" I said, trying my best to keep my voice level and adult-like. "It's not fair that Patrik gets all the change."

My mother looked at my father. Their eyes had a bewildered, deer-in-the-headlights kind of look. They dearly wanted to give us all the spare change in the world, but not at the expense of joining the line of political refugees, who were begging the dour welfare official for extra money at the *Sozial-Amt*.

It was decided that Patrik and I would split the change, and we did. Patrik saved up small amounts of money, and found his reward in Matchbox cars and cones of ice cream. I put my money into a sturdy, white leather handbag. It had white leather fringing and white leather tassels, and it used to be my mother's.

Almost every day I added a few pfennig coins into it. They jingled in the bottom of my handbag at first, and I wrapped them in a cotton handkerchief to still their jingling sound. There were one hundred pfennigs to a mark, and I collected mostly the small one, two, and five-pfennig coins. A twenty-pfennig coin would have been a fine prize.

I carried my white handbag everywhere. I had my mother guard it while I was on the swings or climbers at the park for fear that somebody would steal it. It had the only money I had in the world in it.

"Your bag is so heavy," she said every time, and every time we went, the bag was heavier and heavier.

THE WEEKS carried on until one day the weather broke and the nudists disappeared from their sun-rock perches by the river. We had defected in summer clothing, bringing just a light summer jacket and a sweatshirt each. Bringing warmer clothes for a summer vacation might have tipped the border guard off that we didn't intend to return.

There was a large building on the outskirts of Munich where we could have gone and asked for free clothing, gently used and in excellent condition. Aside from the intrinsic discomfort we felt at the concept of asking for some stranger's excess clothes, there was the language barrier. My mother's German was rudimentary and my father's, even worse.

The welfare official at the Sozial-Amt probably told us to take advantage of this charity as he gave my father our family's food allowance, our alms. And my father accepted the money, not understanding most of the words as his fist wrapped around the bills, his shoulders hunched and cheeks flushed.

He could have gotten more, had he accepted a job. Only menial jobs were available to refugees, though, and taking a job would have meant settling down. My father wasn't ready to settle down. His dream was to go to America, start a company, and become a millionaire.

All four of us trekked to the Social Amt. We always traveled as a family unit, swimming through a foreign sea of pedestrians whose waves crashed in clipped sounds of German all around us.

We took care to never, ever get separated.

As one, we walked through the large brass door and to the right, through the dark hallway, waited, waited for our turn with the dour, unsmiling Sozial-Amt official.

"*Kein Geld,*" my father said in his broken German. "No money."

The man replied slowly.

We did not understand.

The man gesticulated.

I caught the word "school", and sank further into the background.

"*Kein geld,*" my father repeated his mantra.

"*Es ist kalt,*" my mother said. "It is cold."

The official sighed and handed it over with a lecture that was lost on us.

We took the subway to the other side of town, to the cheap American Store. A black American man sold us pants and jackets. My father talked with him in English, a language with which he was more comfortable.

I tried not to stare at the black man.

I had never seen a black man before. He laughed and gave us kids stickers. I decided that he was okay, that all Americans laugh, are generous, and give kids stickers. We were hoping to go to America and I felt reassured.

We were all a lot warmer now. I marveled at the fine fit of my first-ever jeans and relished the feeling of the sheepskin jacket.

We were all outfitted, but the money was gone. October was half over, and the frowning, black haired official at the Sozial-Amt told us, "*Kein Geld.*"

My father pointed to our clothing. "*Kalt,*" he said.

The official began to sputter wordlessly. He might as well have been speaking German.

We went back to our room. The large, old pension building was designed in grander days. The room's opulent walls were closing in on me now, the wild patterns of its four wallpapers writhing, intruding. My parent's voices echoed, and I eavesdropped shamelessly.

"What are we gonna do?" my father said. "He won't give us any money till November."

My mother looked around, her eyes haunted. "That's almost two weeks," she said. "We need to buy food."

I THOUGHT about my white leather handbag. It was fabulously heavy. A few weeks ago it was only half full, but we were allowed to play in water fountains before the weather turned and I found coins in those fountains. Well-dressed, well-fed tourists tossed in the coins for luck.

Idiots, I had thought back then. How could somebody be that wasteful?

Our parents beseeched us to leave the coins alone. "It's embarrassing," they said.

Patrik and I wouldn't relent. Finally, they compromised.

"Don't let anyone see you."

They would sit on a bench, their backs turned to us as if in ignorance, talking, while my brother and I took to fishing those coins out. We had a system going, where I would reach out with my longer hands, chasing the coins toward him from far-flung places. He would then reach down, immersed down to his slim shoulders, and pulled out every single one. Most were pfennigs of some amount. A few were of foreign denominations.

Some were even marks!

Patrik and I split our haul evenly. He had built a formidable Matchbox car collection. I had earned a very heavy purse. Every night before dinner, I spilled its contents onto my bed and counted it, not moving lest the piles of coins topple over on the soft blankets. It became one of my favorite things to do. It gave me a sense of security.

"We have enough food for tomorrow," I heard my mother say quietly. "After that, maybe we could go to the Sozial-Amt again. Maybe you could talk to that man. Don't they have anyone who speaks Czech? Or at least English?"

I saw my father's face grimace. He would hate to go.

In my mind's eye I saw the splendor of a tortoise hair comb, its Spanish intricacy set with brilliant jewels. Maybe even diamonds. I had twenty-five marks and seventy-six pfennigs. I needed only six marks and twenty-four pfennigs more. If I took my fleece jacket off, I could dip into the fountain real fast, while nobody was looking, and fish for a few more coins. Then I could go into the fancy hair shop on Tall Strasse, right off of

Marien Platz. I could just see myself walk in and buy it. My mother thought it looked gauche but I didn't care.

It was beautiful and it would be mine.

My legs carried me toward where my parents sat. "I have twenty-five marks and seventy-four pfennigs," I heard my voice say.

They turned at me and stared.

"Where did you get twenty five marks?" my mother demanded.

"It's all that spare change," I explained. "The pfennigs that Patrik and I get. And diving in the fountains."

They looked at one another.

"You know, the money I am saving for my hair comb," I supplied helpfully.

"That's excellent!" my father beamed, and there was deep approval in his eyes. "We have money again!"

I lifted my head, straightening.

"But… but that's the money I saved. I saved it. I carried it everywhere. I am saving for my hair comb."

"You'd be wasting money," my mother said.

"That money is food on the table," my father said. "We are all in this together. When we have money again, you can get your new hair comb."

My handbag full of coins must have weighed ten pounds when we hauled it to the post office. The postmaster smiled and said something in German. Obviously, he approved of youngsters that saved. He counted the coins in a machine and handed me several crisp bills.

They were not brand new, but the machine made them smooth. Full of promise.

I handed them over to my father. The postmaster raised his eyebrows, and I smiled at him.

As though I was a regular kid.

As though everything was all right.

We were able to buy bread and rice and liver and wine until the end of October. In November, our family received an official U.S. political asylum, and with the asylum came a generous financial stipend.

Food was more plentiful now, and there was enough money left over to stop in that fancy hair shop on Tall Strasse. I yearned for my carved Spanish hair comb, carved of shiny tortoise shell and beset with jewels.

My mother steered me in the direction of a modest hair clip that had a few rhinestones in it. At seven marks and fifty pfennigs, it set us back an equivalent of a rotisserie chicken, one package of American bread, and four apples. I hefted it. It was light.

It was made of cheap plastic. The stones were no jewels at all.

"Are you sure this is worth it?" my mother asked.

I recalled all those times she and Dad sat on the bench with their back turned, while Patrik and I searched for the furthest, biggest coins we could get.

It was now a matter of principle.

I straightened up and forced a smile as genuine as the hairclip itself. "It's beautiful," I said.

Chapter 5

SMOKE AND SHADOWS

November 23rd, 1979, Munich, West Germany (Penzion Beck)

JUST WHEN I thought we would live in a cheap penzion forever and I would never, ever go to school again, my father returned from a solitary outing. I remember it being solitary because we had to stay in our room, doors locked. My father returned after several hours of nervous waiting. He knocked on the door and said the password, and my mother let him in.

His face was aglow with excitement.

"They really are there," he said to her. "It's amazing what good propaganda can do."

My mother put a pot of water on the small electric burner and prepared two cups with instant coffee powder and sugar, condensed milk waiting by the side.

"20 Possart Strasse," he said, grinning like a kid at Christmas. "Just like they said. A true nest of imperialist conspiracy."

His enthusiasm was infectious. I edged my way over and gingerly sat at the square formica table. My face voiced questions I did not dare ask. Such as, where have you been and how did it go?

My mother offered me a cup of tea, thus including me in adult conversation. I hunched over its steam gratefully, my ears strained to the breaking point.

"Straighten up," my father told me. When I did, he turned toward my mother.

"I don't know how I remembered this," he said. "Sometimes people remember the strangest things, but I remember watching one of those stupid government propaganda shows on TV, you know, in Prague."

He tipped the tin can to stir more condensed milk into his coffee.

"Anyhow, they were talking about a subversive, anti-patriotic organization called the American Fund for Czechoslovak Refugees, based here in Munich. They even showed the building it was in, and I remember seeing the sign; it said 20 Possart Strasse. So I looked it up on the map. It's not too far from here if you cut across the park. Anyhow, I decided it's time for us to get subverted."

"What are those people like," my mother asked in a flat voice, stirring her own coffee.

"There is an old man, a Czech-American. He runs the show. He gave me a little bit of money to tide us over… Made an appointment for me."

"An appointment?" my mother asked.

"With the Americans. There will be some interviews, because the Americans will give political asylum only to some people. This is a strong year for refugees like us, so there is competition. But they like the fact that I am a scientist. I think this will work out."

"What if the Americans decide they don't want us?" I asked.

"Then we'll probably stay here, in Germany."

I hoped we wouldn't have to stay in Germany. I didn't want to go to a German school and learn German and be made fun of. There was a Czech couple we heard of who lived in Germany for many years. Their daughter was born here. She was an official German, with citizenship and everything. She spoke German without an accent. Even her Czech was bad, because she only spoke it at home.

Because she had Czech parents, though, her teacher made her sit in the back of the class with all the Turkish kids that didn't speak German at all. She let her sit with the others only once her parents raised a stink and showed their German citizenship papers.

In Germany, I would always be a foreigner, *Auslander*.

In America, though, anyone could become an American; everyone got the same chances, no matter what the Czechoslovak state propaganda had to say about it.

FROM THEN on, my father was gone for a few hours each day, handling numerous and lengthy interrogations. The Americans decided we were keepers: a prominent scientist with a nice family. We still worried, however, because the Czech secret police tried to get a bead on our location. That was, after all, their standard operating procedure. Every so often we would spot a tail, and then zig and zag through the crowd to lose him. It was always a younger guy. Could be, it was just a coincidence and we were jumping at shadows. Then again, could be, he was paid by the Czechs to follow us and report on our movements. Stories of people being dragged back were not uncommon.

I was scared. I didn't want to be kidnapped by the Czechs and dragged back. I didn't want to be tortured in some nameless prison.

"You'd be fine; you're just a kid," my father would say. "And that's why we're going to America. Americans would never torture prisoners."

"That's why we speak only German in public, and always walk together," my mother reminded me. "We don't want to be identified as Czechs. You never know who might be listening."

"Mother says she's got a visa; they are allowing her to visit us here in Munich for a few days," my mother said few days later, after one of our rare telephone calls to Prague. The four of us pushed our way out of the yellow telephone booth. Brisk autumn air washed over me.

"She said she will come and try to convince us to return," my mother said.

"You think?" my father asked.

"No. I think she is bringing us winter clothing," she continued. "And she misses us."

MY FATHER met my grandmother at the train station alone.

"They will put a tail on her to see where we are," he said. "It's better if I go alone."

My father used to be an Olympic-level boxer, and few weeks after we ended up in Munich, he accosted a fellow tailing us.

He took him around the corner for a brief conversation.

We weren't tailed after that anymore.

He swore that he didn't do anything to him, but I always pictured him executing the jab-jab-right cross combination he taught me when I was younger. Right on the side of the jaw for maximum concussive power.

We waited in endless stillness. The room was straightened up, the food and drink sat at the ready. Mother exuded nervous energy which she could ill afford to expend.

Hearing the laborious bumping of my grandmother's

luggage up the stairs felt like a release.

My father knocked on the door and said the password.

My mother unlocked.

"There you are! Katerina, you grew so much! Patrik! I missed all of you." My grandmother entered the room, possessing the space around her, her great chest like the prow of a ship. The space was filled with words and emotions and I wanted to retreat from all that noise, soften the intensity of it all. But if I retired I'd miss all the adult conversation, so I steeled myself against the onslaught of feelings, and stayed. Seated at the little table, I was nigh invisible.

She greeted us all with her large embrace. When my turn came, she looked up into my eyes.

"And whatever happened to my little girl? You look like they would let you have a glass of wine at just about any restaurant." Her gaze measured me up and down and I felt oddly self-conscious. "Too bad I don't have a sewing machine." She turned to my mother. "I brought your old bras for her, but I don't think they will fit anymore."

Before I could feel entirely mortified at her open observations, she began to unpack all the things she had brought—and there was a lot.

"And here I brought your winter jackets," she said, adding my mother's black fur winter coat to the formidable pile.

"I didn't bring shoes for the children." She inclined her head toward my mother apologetically. "They probably don't fit anymore anyhow."

Her own possessions amounted to mere two changes of clothing. Most of the two suitcases and two satchels contained things for us.

"And now for the good part," she said, and undid the buttons of her coatdress.

My father stirred uncomfortably.

I grinned.

"See what a good smuggler I am? I am so good! Look what I managed to bring through the checkpoint!" She flipped the front of her bra where the little triangle connected the cups. On the inside, stitched down with white thread, was a pair of ruby and diamond earrings.

"I know your ears aren't pierced," she said to my mother. "Katerina may pierce hers someday." Looking at me, she said, "These belonged to your grandfather's grandmother." She pulled our birth certificates out of her girdle, and an original oil painting by Slavicek from a double-bottomed bag. There was more jewelry for my mother.

"I brought you all I could," she said, chin in the air. "We miss you so much. Grandpa too. Even that dog misses you." She sniffled, reached into her pocket, and pulled out a cotton handkerchief to wipe her nose.

"And now I have to tell you how your husband fooled the tail they put on me." She regaled us with a blow-by-blow account.

"And I thought it was him all along. A young guy in an old jacket like that had no business in a first class car. Where would he get the money?"

When they had entered a subway car, the young guy in the old jacket had followed them, entering the packed subway car through another door. But Munich subway cars have a door on each side; you can walk right through from one platform to the other. Right before the doors closed, my father and grandmother, luggage and all, jumped out the door on the opposite side. The young man in the old jacket was seen heading for a far-away Munich suburb.

"And you should have seen his long face, pressed against the window," crowed my grandmother victoriously.

Nothing like getting some egg on the face of the enemy.

We all laughed, and my father opened a three-liter bottle of wine. I was often sent to a store across the street to buy the necessities: bread, wine, and cigarettes. It was a grownup job, and now they trusted me with it.

"*Ein Madchentrauben, bitte, zwei Marlborough Cigaretten, und ein Bröt,*" I would say, glowing with pride, twice a week. The two older ladies behind the counter store would look at one another, then grace me with a kind smile. They would hand me two packages of cigarettes, a three-liter bottle of jug wine, and a loaf of bread. And now, my parents and my grandmother clinked cheap hotel glasses with their cheap muscatel wine and I knew that I was excused from further conversation for a little while.

MY FATHER was at interrogations with the Americans again, although we didn't tell Grandmother that. What she didn't know wouldn't hurt her. My mother was dressed in her skirt and walking shoes, waiting for us impatiently, organizing, cajoling. But I had nothing to wear.

"The child can't walk around like that," my grandmother declared. "Look at her. At least we could go to Kaufhof and buy her a new bra."

My mother hissed.

"Really," my grandmother barged on, choosing to be oblivious. "Did you have that conversation with her yet?"

"This is not the time to speak of this," my mother answered sharply.

They were arguing, and they were arguing over me and my upbringing. It was a well-worn path. My grandmother had strong opinions, my mother had strong inhibitions.

"She is old enough to know certain things. Just look

at her."

"She isn't fourteen yet." My mother's voice brooked no argument. I vaguely recalled the autumn of the previous year—my menarche came on my birthday. My grandmother wanted my mother to have a conversation about the facts of life with me. My mother flatly refused.

I remember having been in my grandmother's kitchen the summer of the previous year.

"Why can't you tell me about the facts of life, Grandma," I said. I always felt I could talk to her about absolutely anything.

"It is not my place," she had pronounced with great formality. She was stirring a pot of tart, fragrant plum preserves, her eyes not meeting mine. "Your mother has declared that she does not wish me to speak to you of these things, even though I have offered. You will just have to wait." She had sighed back then and stirred some more, before she turned to face me again.

"If you're patient, I'll let you lick the mixing spoon." It was an old bribe that had outlived its usefulness, but I nodded, knowing my acquiescence would please her.

And here we were again, one year later. My mother and my grandmother were embroiled in the same struggle as before, and I idly wondered what, exactly, did they mean by the 'facts of life'.

"We seem to have new neighbors," my mother announced. "Two men." The room next to us was finally occupied. We shared the hallway bathroom with them. Their door was always open, and their radio played rock'n'roll. Whenever we made ready to go out, they were going out too. We wore our Prague jackets; they wore tan trench coats. When we came back, they showed up fifteen minutes after us.

"The Americans didn't like your mother's visiting," my

father said out of grandmother's earshot.

"I bet they are Americans," my mother said. When I tried to say hello to them, she shushed me and pulled me back. "Don't talk to strangers. You don't know who they are."

I didn't know who they were but I had a pretty good idea. I slept better at night. Czech prison cells no longer haunted my dreams.

Chapter 6

THE CARELESS REFUGEE LIFE

November 28th, 1979, Munich, West Germany (Secret Location)

BY THE END of November, a space opened up at the barracks. Our family moved from Penzion Beck to an American facility full of Eastern Bloc refugees. The three-bedroom efficiency apartment was a definite step up in accommodations. Meals were served three times a day, and there was an allowance to cover our personal purchases.

Our family no longer needed to beg at the Sozial-Amt. We were coming to America—as soon as our turn came. My father was interrogated daily, answering the same questions over and over. His caseworker tried to speak Czech. "*Pozdravujte vaše rodidla*", he once said, trying to say, "Say hello to your family." We laughed and laughed—he had told Father to send regards to his vagina. Little did we know how hard English would be for us only two months hence.

THE THIRD bedroom of our suite was occupied by Stefan from Romania, who was twenty-four, tall and polite and swarthy. We became acquainted with a number of political refugees—two Czech men, a Czechoslovak Air Force pilot with his wife and child, a Romanian father and daughter and the daughter's lover, and a Russian mother and her sixteen-year old daughter. The Russian daughter got to go out to clubs with the Czech men, and I envied her.

"You don't want to be like her," my mother said after word spread that the guys got her stripped down to her underwear in the back of the car. "That's indecent. You would get a reputation."

"What kind of a reputation?" I asked eagerly. This was grown-up territory, and it was data acquisition time.

My mother looked at me, then through me.

"You are so naïve," she said, and tapped the ash off her cigarette. "You don't know anything."

"Well then tell me, and I won't be naïve anymore," I replied sensibly. It was too bad I was told to stay away from the Russian girl. She was reasonably close to my age, and I spoke a bit of Russian. There was nobody else.

I missed school. There had been a whole social network in our class of thirty-two students. We started first grade together and moved on as a unit. We traded information. I found out about at least some of the workings of the female body from my schoolmates, and a good thing too, because I sure wasn't told anything at home. By now, they all surely knew the 'facts of life.' I wasn't there to listen in and find out about Martina's sister, and what she had to say about her adventures with boys.

There were benefits to life without school obligations, though. I learned to fit into adult company. When they drank, I sat at the corner of the table, away from the door so it was more awkward for my parents to send me away. I sipped my Coca Cola, dodging their cigarette smoke as best as I could. I laughed when they laughed, and I remained silent when they spoke of adult things.

ONCE AGAIN, I asked my mother to tell me about the 'facts of life'.

"Not with Patrik around. Even you are too young for these things." Her voice was aloof, uncomfortable. She walked to the window and looked outside at the German families streaming out of a church, dressed in their good Sunday clothes. They had lives. Regular lives. She sighed.

"Get dressed, Patrik too," she said. "We're going for a walk."

We sauntered to a playground nearby. Patrik and I played while she sat alone and smoked, ever watchful for approaching strangers, for suspicious cars.

Monotonous days of the refugee social life were lubricated with inexpensive wine, drunk liberally and often. What other way to spend time? What other way to release stress? Everyone was waiting for the word.

"They said another month," somebody said. "They said I will go to California, but this is a strong year for refugees. Their offices are swamped."

"The Iranians are keeping them busy," someone remarked.

"We are lucky to be here, and not in Italy," said Josef, a grizzled veteran of the refugee process. "The Italians won't give you anything. You're stuck in a refugee camp right on the border. Took me months to get out of there." He took a drink of his jug wine. "And the things I have seen…" He glanced in my direction.

I wanted to know what he had seen, but he changed the subject. "Anyway, Germany is the way to go. The welfare system here is great. Have you been to that warehouse with free clothing?" My parents shook their heads, their expressions pained.

"The Germans give perfectly good things away, for free!" Joseph said. "They could resell it, but they don't even bother. That's how rich they are. And the Germans are meticulous. You take a television from someone, it's clean. Not a speck of dust. You know it will work."

I gasped. A television. Our family was the last in my class to have a television. It cost a fortune and played black-and-white programs on two channels.

"The thing to do is to become a refugee in one country, use up your allowance, then move to another country," he explained. "This is good, but we'll have to move on pretty soon. We have been here too long. The Americans want us to go to the US, and the Germans won't give us any more money unless we take one of those menial jobs." Joseph's audience rumbled. The room was full of educated people. A job sweeping monkey shit in a zoo would be a demeaning waste of time.

Two weeks later, I watched Joseph and his friend manufacture fake Yugoslav passports at our dinner table. The atmosphere was thick with cigarette smoke and adventure as everyone took part in the illicit process. Ubiquitous glasses of cheap wine or hard liquor mingled with spare photographs, grommets, nail files, and glue. Two Yugoslav passports, presumably stolen and resold, were getting a makeover. If everyone did a good job, nobody in Holland would notice the original photos were carefully replaced by instant-booth Polaroids.

The two men pocketed their passports. They stayed just long enough to draw the next week's personal allowance.

"No loss there," my parents agreed as they discussed their disappearance. "They were probably Czech spies anyway. They knew the system too well."

Western countries extended generous help to Eastern Bloc refugees during the Cold War. A few con men always took advantage of these systems. Our cohabitants might have been branded as refugees by the Germans or the Italians, but we trusted no one. Most especially, we didn't trust our fellow Czechs.

It was brisk outside and three inches of snow covered the streets. It didn't matter much on a Saturday. The stores were closed anyway. We were taking a walk, a welcome opportunity to get out of the barracks, away from the smoke, from the people. We passed the used-car lot where our powder blue Skoda-100 sat, waiting for a buyer.

"Well, she took us far, that's for certain," my father said, looking at the snow-covered car nostalgically. "At least we got twenty marks for her."

Gasoline was expensive, public transportation was cheap. The car soon became a liability.

"Mila has a car, though," I said. He was a younger Czech guy and drove a sporty yellow number. I was envious. Even a reconstructed, powder blue Skoda would have been better than nothing.

"I wonder where he gets the money for the upkeep," my mother remarked. "It's not like the Americans are giving him enough money for a car.

My father looked thoughtful. "He may be playing the Germans for money at the same time," he said.

"How, though? Doesn't he have to tell them he is with the Americans now?"

"Well, yes, he does," my father said, "but suppose he spells his name a little differently. It will take a long time to find out he's not two people, and by the time the fraud is discovered, he'll be gone."

"But other people have a lot more than we do, too, and they get money only from the Americans," I said. "Like the pilot's wife. Mom, have you been in their bathroom?"

"Yes, and I've seen all those bottles of nail polish." There were forty, fifty of them, in tidy rows sorted by color, with lipsticks to match.

"I don't think she paid for those, dear," my mother said delicately.

"What do you mean?"

"Your mother means to say that some people steal when they go to the stores. It's a bad thing to do. It gives all immigrants a bad name. Didn't you see how the shopkeepers watch us carefully?"

I learned a lot on our Saturday walks around town. Here, they played along with the refugee community, pretended to forge friendships, yet trusting no one. Inside their homes they would speak freely, and say only politically neutral, socially acceptable things in public. My parents were as fork-tongued as they were back in Czechoslovakia, and I followed suit. In private, they engaged in targeted character autopsy.

"Did you know she was sleeping around behind his back?"

"Did you know he did drugs in Holland?"

"Do you think she makes money on the side? You know, in clubs?"

"Do you think he's an agent?"

"Did you hear she's pregnant?"

"Did you hear she has a sugar daddy?"

I was sure these comments, uttered on the side in that special secret language of long-married couples, had something to do with the elusive 'facts of life'. Yet there was never a good time to broach the subject. It never felt right to do so in my father's company. It never felt right to do in my brother's company either. My mother and I were hardly ever alone.

THE YOUNG Romanian fellow, Stefan, liked to play cars and blocks with my brother in the living room while the very young Michael Jackson danced on German television. He was the only person who would talk to me for just for company's sake, and I enjoyed Stefan's attentions. I sure wasn't going to be stripped in the back of the car like that Russian girl, but… some attention was nice. My father was in interrogations most of the workday. My mother was often alone in their room, the door closed. Stefan didn't speak nearly as much Russian as I did, but he knew Italian, and I knew a few words. A smattering of that, and some German, and a lot of gesticulation provided for a conversation of sorts.

My 14th birthday rolled around.

"We thought you should get something special this year," my father announced as we stood in front of the very small, very old shop window. "You really wanted that hair comb, and it looked so fancy in the window. Here, though, you can choose something fancy that has lasting value."

I looked from my father to my mother and back in disbelief.

"And we can do this?" I asked.

"We were able to save some money. Not much… but enough."

The store window display was encrusted with red garnets. Rings next to rings, thick bangle bracelets, pendants, earrings, intricate Victorian necklaces intended for elegant evenings. They were all old, and beautiful.

We left the store happy, I with a garnet ring on my finger. It was large enough to be noticed but small enough to wear every day. It was gold-filled silver. Gold-filled. I never had a single thing with real gold on it before.

Stefan didn't forget my birthday either. He put a gold ring with an Egyptian coin on my finger. Then he bent over my face and kissed me. I sat there, both stunned and pleased. When his tongue penetrated my lips, confusion gripped me. Was that the famous "French kiss" my friends were talking about last year, or… ?

He slipped his hand under my shirt, up to my breast.

I didn't know what to do. It felt grown-up and confusing at the same time. The grown-up part stroked my ego, but the confusion stilled me with sudden, unfamiliar fear.

"*Cara mia*," he said. "*Mia amore*." I didn't know what to do. If I told my parents, knowing what they thought of other people who behaved in a certain way, I was sure there would be hell to pay. I extricated myself.

"*Danke shön*," I said, spreading my finger and redirecting attention at the ring. Getting something so valuable pleased me. This ring was worth two whole handbags full of coins from the water fountains. I saw one like it sold at Marienplatz for forty-five marks.

Yet I was confused by his desire to touch me. *Maybe Romanians do that sort of a thing*, I thought.

We were told we would leave for America in three weeks, but Stefan was told his flight would leave in three days. He didn't have much to pack.

"Poor guy," my mother had said the next day. "He is so lonely."

My parents knew of the ring.

"If there was anything going on, I would have put a stop to that," she said proudly to all who would listen.

The day before Stefan was to leave, he turned the ring on my finger so it looked like a wedding band.

"*Prego*." His eyes met mine with dark intensity.

Oh, he is proposing marriage. But I am too young.

"*In America*," I said, struggling with my fledgling Italian.

He shook his head, pointed at his watch, and indicated he will expect me after midnight. His hand wandered under my shirt and bra. The concept of personal boundaries unknown to me, I nodded my head. After all, why not? He just wants to spend some time. He wants to marry in America. It won't happen, of course, but poor guy, he looks so lonely. He's nervous before his big flight.

What's the harm, keeping him company?

He saw me nod and his smile brightened.

PROMISES SHOULD be kept. I had every intention of meeting Stefan that night, but to do so, I needed a clear coast. My brother decided not to sleep. Christmas was coming and he was wound up with too much chocolate.

My parents were late to turn in.

"Stop being so loud," I heard my father's voice through the wall. "You'll wake the children."

There was some crashing about.

"I don't want to go to America!" my mother screamed.

"We already discussed this. We already decided," my father said. His voice was desperate, pleading.

There was a sound of objects thrown. There was yelling.

"Stop that, or somebody will hear you," my father hissed. "Just be quiet."

"I am going back home!" my mother sobbed. "I am going back to Prague!"

"There is nothing for us there. Just jail. Think of the children."

"I am going! I am not staying here, with the Germans!"

I heard a key turn in the lock of their door.

"You are staying. Go to sleep and sober up, it will be all better in the morning," my father said in a voice I heard him use with me sometimes. It was a voice which promised better things tomorrow if I will only be good today.

My wristwatch showed two o'clock when I finally decided to turn in, and my fatigue helped me fall asleep deeply enough not to hear my parents war in the adjoining room.

Stefan was packed and ready to go. Lacking enough words in Italian, I tried to express the events of last night in Russian.

"*Italiano,*" he said stubbornly.

"*Pardone. Parenti.*" I gesticulated madly. Not sleeping, waiting, expressing regrets.

His bearded face darkened and his brow furrowed in anger. He said something in Italian.

"*No comprende,*" I said.

He said more. He reached for my hand and tried to take the gold ring off my finger. I closed my fingers in a tight fist.

"*No!*" I said firmly. A kernel of understanding began to dawn on me. I was still hazy on the mechanical and physiological details of life, but it was now clear that he didn't have what people in old books used to call "honorable intentions".

"*Puta*," he said, spitting the word out. I didn't know what that meant. I smiled a conciliatory smile. My brother came out, attracted by the activity. He looked at me, then honed in on Stefan.

"Will you play cars with me?" he asked in Czech, pointing to his Matchbox car collection.

Chapter 7

SMOOTH LANDING, ROUGH SUR-

January 18th, 1980, Walnut Lane, Princeton, New Jersey, USA

MY BROTHER Patrik was excited to cross the Atlantic in Lufthansa's Boeing 747 because it was the largest plane available. I was excited to cross the Atlantic in Lufthansa's Boeing 747 because it went in the right direction: West.

"If the Soviets and the Americans go at it, this place will be a battlefield," my father said back in Munich. "So will Czechoslovakia. And if it's a nuclear war, the farther away we are, the better." My mother agreed.

I remembered my sixth grade Civil Defense teacher, Mr. Otomansky, explaining how to extinguish napalm by throwing sand on it. He helped us fit our new, larger gas masks to our growing heads. The new model didn't have the elephant trunk like the one we'd been issued in first grade. He taught us first aid and azimuth orientation, and he supervised our first firing of a VZ 50 submachine gun at a nearby military base. He told us how to recognize various nerve agents and what to do about them. But when it came to being nuked, even the capable Mr. Otomansky—with all his compulsory military education—had little to say.

Nuclear war was never a serious concern for me, just like paying the electric bill wasn't a serious concern. Both were an abstract concept of the adult realm. Both were threatening. Both were to be avoided.

But going to America! That was a dream come true. Only a year ago, I'd talked with my friends about our hopes for the future.

"Where will you defect to when you grow up?" someone asked.

"Germany," said Iveta. She'd studied German for years and was already fluent, she sewed her own clothes, and she took care of her little brother. Iveta could do anything in the world.

"Probably Italy. I have an aunt there," said Veronika. I could see the dark-haired Veronika somewhere in the Mediterranean, baking her famous cakes, and supervising someone – anyone – into doing just about anything. I envied her the people skills I so sorely lacked.

"I will defect to America," I said, trying to feel halfway competent in face of my half-baked plan. Grandma sewed my clothes and she did the baking, but at least I could aim to escape the furthest.

"All you're interested in are the Indians." The girls laughed.

I blushed. It was absolutely true—influenced by Fennimore Cooper and Karl May, I often envisioned myself on horseback, trekking through the prairie with a gun slung off the pommel of my saddle.

"No, really, I want to go there," I diverted the talk from my obsession with Indians. I hesitated for a second. This was classified information—something not to be spoken of outside of the family. Yet Veronika baked a marbled bundt all by herself last year, and Iveta was standing there wearing American-style corduroys she sewed with her own hands. And you couldn't tell they weren't imported.

Insecurity won over prudence.

"My father was there for two months once," I said.

"Don't tell anyone, but he said it was good. Really good."

They leaned in toward me, conspiratorial and curious.

"It's not like they tell us here," I continued, secure in my spotlight. "Americans don't have slavery anymore. Everybody's equal. And those pimps and prostitutes and drugs they write about in the papers here, those are only in small areas of big cities. In the rest of the country, people are normal. Like us. They live in nice houses and go to work and to school."

Their ears pricked up. This was real intel, the words of a daughter whose father had been there and had seen it and told her all about it.

This was the real thing.

"And you know what else they have there? They have machines for toasting bread."

"Get out!" Iveta exclaimed in disbelief.

"No, he told me years ago. He told me that in each home there is this little machine, and in the morning, people put slices of bread into it, push a button, and the bread jumps out when it's done. I remember it because I called him a liar and didn't get in trouble for it."

Calling a parent a liar was a corporal punishment spanking offense, but that one time, when I had really meant it, nothing had come of it. I really thought he was pulling my leg. Why would anyone build a machine just for toasting bread? What a wasteful idea. How naïve did he think I was?

He'd only looked sad. He had looked past me back then, with his shoulders drooped into an uncharacteristic slump.

"Don't believe me if you don't want to, he'd said. But they are called 'toasters', and they really do exist."

And now we were flying to America, to the land where normal people lived in normal houses, where everybody was free and had equal opportunities, and where everyone had their own toaster.

WE WERE ushered through the empty catacombs of the JFK Airport in New York. It was late at night. There were officials to talk to and papers to sign, and my eyes drooped with my first-ever jetlag.

"There you are! I was getting worried," said Mr. Kliment, excited. He was a former colleague of my father from Prague, a fellow hydrogel scientist. He loaded the four of us and our two suitcases into a brown Chevrolet Impala and headed down the New Jersey Turnpike toward Princeton.

"We are in New Jersey now," he said. "It's another state." Another state, yet the border was invisible, with no passports required.

"It's terrible how this area has gotten crowded," Mr. Kliment narrated our journey toward Princeton. I plastered my face against the cold glass of the rear passenger window. The utility poles and trees were flashing by, barely visible against the inky sky. The land was deserted. Vast forests of trees that lined the highway opened out periodically, showing clusters of lights and buildings.

"That's New Brunswick," Mr. Kliment said. "Almost there."

So this was America and her most populated coast. And yet there were trees, there was emptiness. I inhaled the stale car air, feeling the expansiveness of the air on the other side of the window. If the land was this empty, maybe there were still Indians nearby.

THE KLIMENTS lived in a split-level, three-bedroom house and they shared it with us freely. Patrik and I slept in their son's room, their son slept on the sofa in the den. My parents slept in their daughter's room while their daughter was away in college. We were introduced to the local Czech-American community, and to a number of American friends.

The house was palatial. Mrs. Kliment impressed upon me that her fifteen-year-old son gave up his own room for us, a room which housed his own television. A television, which he bought with his own money. I didn't understand how a boy only a year older than I could have amassed enough money to buy a television.

Sacrifices were made all around. Mrs. Kliment cooked for twice the number of people than before, and her meals were exotic.

"This is called 'lasagna'," she said. "It's the latest thing. I got the recipe from Maureen."

They ate their meals in the wrong order, salad first instead of last. They held their utensils wrong, too—the fork in the right hand, spearing precut meat and vegetables. I tried to conform.

"May I help?" I asked about one week later, as Mrs. Kliment and my mom and I milled around in the kitchen. My help was sure to be turned down; I never got to help in the kitchen in Prague. Foodstuffs couldn't be wasted on beginner cooks.

"Sure, just dump the rice from this pot, here, into this bowl," said Mrs. Kliment.

I missed and dumped half of the rice in the sink. I was mortified. That was enough to feed our whole family.

Mrs. Kliment swooped by with a diplomatic smile. She spooned the rice from the sink into the serving bowl.

"The kitchen sink is supposed to be the cleanest place in the house," she said in a level voice, daring anyone to disagree. "And besides, nobody needs to know." She looked at me encouragingly as my mother cringed with embarrassment behind her. I nodded.

Once we were seated, I watched her serve the rice as though nothing had happened. A sudden need to confess my sins came over me. As though she could tell, she smiled firmly across the table and shook her head. 'We have a secret together,' her eyes seemed to say. 'No need to speak.'

ON MY THIRD day in America, I was told it was time to go to school.

"She is so mature," the Kliments said. "She may not fit with the Junior High students. She'd be there for only one semester anyway."

"She is too intelligent to miss a whole year like this," my father said, his expression regretful. "She finished seventh grade in Prague."

"She'll need to learn English one way or another. At this point, nobody will be able to tell which grade she should be in," Mr. Kliment said. "Let her go straight to high school."

Thus, after seven month of idleness, I was skipped forward a year to enter the second term of ninth grade at the busy, tumultuous Princeton High School.

WE SAT in the counselor's office.

"Her name is Dr. Thompson," my father said in Czech. "Thompson, like the British submachine gun. Easy to remember."

Dr. Thompson was a small lady with steel-gray hair. She picked my courses for me, then looked in my eyes for the first time.

"This will be a good beginning," she said slowly.

I looked toward my father questioningly. I didn't understand.

"Look it up! Here, I brought you a dictionary," he said.

I hefted the heavy English-Czech, Czech-English dictionary. Its title gleamed from its blue plastic cover.

"It will be a good beginning," Dr. Thompson said again, patiently.

The last word was the one I didn't yet understand. Laboriously, with everyone looking on, I fumbled my way to the English-to-Czech section. Up in the B's, I found the alien word. It looked different than it sounded, but when I pointed it to my father, he nodded.

I smiled at her.

"Yes. Good beginning," I said. It was good enough for starters.

THE MOST exciting thing about America was that everyone was equal. Everyone had the same opportunities. If you went to school and worked hard, it would pay off. Once you were fifteen, you could even get a job after school.

Students at Princeton High were tracked according to their proficiency in various subjects, and I was put into the slowest track for everything because I didn't speak any English. My counselor took me to a small classroom. I was the only white person there.

Was this a mistake? Was I in a classroom for negroes? I wanted to ask, but did not know how.

The teacher introduced me. She taught grammar and she was white-skinned, with dark curly hair and prominent teeth. The students were full of uncontained energy, jumping in their seats, calling out. I sat quietly, observing, trying to figure out their rules. Another teacher walked into the classroom.

I stood at attention.

That was what you did when a teacher entered the room, or if you were called on. It was important to show respect to teachers, and to your elders.

No one else stood. The teachers looked at me to see what I would do. I did nothing, waiting for permission to be seated again. Eventually one of them gesticulated, and I sat back down onto the hard wooden chair.

My classmates were wild with excitement at my actions. Their jumping around resembled Brownian motion. They shot out questions in incomprehensible bursts, and got answers I didn't understand.

I learned not to stand up.

My *English As Foreign Language* class was full of immigrants. I sat in the middle and to the left, uncomfortable with people sitting behind me. I wanted to see all these people, people who came from all corners of the world, and who didn't speak any more English than I did.

A German girl and I represented Europe. There were two girls from Guatemala and one girl from Japan. The rest of the students were boat people from Southeast Asia who knew one another and spoke with each other in Chinese on the sly, and several refugees from Haiti who sat with silent, gleaming smiles and stark, ebony skin.

We were all in it together.

We helped one another with conversation exercises. We slowly made progress. And we made friends.

Mai was three years older than I, but she'd missed a lot of school while her family was stuck in a refugee camp in Thailand. She flashed me her kind smile, one of her teeth gold and black with old repairs. Our English had to improve considerably before I understood how fortunate I was compared to her.

She had a mother, and brothers, and sisters, but no father. It came out in one of those neutral language exercises where we talked about family structure and how to say "mother" and "father" and words like that. As she struggled with her dictionary, we also learned the word "dead," and "starved," and "on a boat."

I fingered the free lunch ticket in my pocket. I was so fortunate.

We had it so easy. If push came to shove, Munich was full of water-fountains filled with coins.

THE THING about learning a language is that you can always say more than you can understand. My first day of school drove that home nice and hard. The school building was a nice, neo-gothic structure with ivy-covered turrets, secret passages that connected the numerous wings, and more doors than I knew what to do with.

A stream of students carried me out like so much flotsam on bobbing waves. I ended up on a concrete sidewalk by a frostbitten lawn.

I looked around.

Nothing around me looked even remotely familiar.

Somehow, I ended up on the wrong side of the building and saw wrong streets and wrong trees, and I had absolutely no idea how to get back to the Kliment house. There I was, me and my dictionary and no money and new in the country, and lost on my first day out.

Forget embarrassed—I was terrified.

Suppressing panic, I pulled the dictionary out of my backpack. I constructed a sentence and wrote it down on a lined yellow pad. Then I practiced reading it.

Once I could read the unfamiliar words smoothly enough, I scanned the streams of students walking to their homes, searching for a kindly soul.

My eyes drifted to a girl about my size and age. She

didn't seem in too much of a hurry, and she seemed kind, so I approached her.

"Excuse me, please, where is three two one Walnut Lane?" I read off my paper.

She looked at me with surprise. People don't come up and read a question off a lined yellow pad every day.

She asked me a question.

I thought about the sounds she made, but none seemed familiar. With a corner of my mind I thought I should have been embarrassed, but a louder voice drowned the thought out. This was no time for bashful embarrassment—making myself understood became a matter of survival. I shrugged apologetically, and read my sentence again.

"Excuse me please, where is 321 Walnut Lane?"

She spied the dictionary under my arm. Not wasting time asking my permission, she pulled it out and, using the English-Czech part, she found the Czech equivalent for "lost".

"Yes, I am lost," I said carefully.

She read my sentence carefully, took me by my hand, and led me three blocks down the street to the right house. She rang the doorbell and handed me over to the surprised Mrs. Kliment.

I carried that dictionary under my arm for a full two years.

MY MOTHER stayed home with Patrik. Mrs. Kliment would take them shopping and to the park in her Impala. My father was busy looking for a job.

"We need to get out of here. We need to stand on our own feet," he would say.

"We are in the way. It's been three weeks already," my mother said, concerned. "I hate to impose." She said it in a loud conversational voice so the young daughter, visiting from college, would hear. The word would spread that we didn't intend to set root. Our extended presence was beginning to be felt in little daily disasters and impositions, like our lack of seasonal clothing.

"You have nothing to wear," Mrs. Kliment told me. She surveyed my dark brown polyester skirt and my brown-and-white polyester top. It was my best outfit.

I bristled.

"My grandmother made this skirt. It's a good skirt."

I saw my mother gesticulate from behind, alarm apparent in her eyes. I was not to disagree.

"Well… it is a very good skirt," Mrs. Kliment allowed. "But don't you think a girl like yourself should have more changes of clothing?" She turned to my mother. "I need to go to the mall anyway. I will take her along."

My mother flopped her arms about helplessly. She couldn't say no—I needed the clothing. She couldn't say yes—we couldn't afford it.

"Don't worry. They have those after-Christmas sales, so it's a special gift. I love shopping, don't you?"

Later that night, I sat at the dinner table in my new pants and a turtleneck.

"I talked to some investors while you were still in Germany," Mr. Kliment said in the direction of my father. "They are interested, but they want to be involved."

My father was a prodigy in the field of hydrogel chemistry, where the Czechs led almost all the rest of the world. He and his father were on the team that developed the first soft contact lenses. The ancient sage of the field was Dr. Otto Wichterle. My dad was the hot young buck. For a while he'd worked for another chemist, before his boss had defected. That was our sponsor, Mr. Kliment.

The Czechoslovak government had sold the contact lens patents to a small American company, which couldn't bring them to market. They sold the invention on to Bausch & Lomb, which did. By now my father considered those original lenses to be almost stone age science in light of all the new advances he'd made. He had fantastic ideas, and matched his considerable talents with skill, experience, and ambition. The natural thing to do was to start a company.

Mr. Kliment was helping him to set the business up. He'd found some potential investors, but it was slow going.

"That's still not enough to pay both me and the staff we'll need," my father said glumly, surveying the investment proposal. "It's better than nothing, though. I'll just have to take it and work another job on the side."

"We are standing by to help you." Mr. Kliment was as fully caught up as my father by the spirit of entrepreneurial adventure, of the American Dream. Surely they could all work together again. Surely now that my father was in the States, they could all make their fortune. It would take some work, but what didn't?

Six weeks after we landed in America, my father landed a job.

Chapter 8

IN VINO VERITAS

April 17th, 1980, Jefferson Road, Princeton, New Jersey, USA

MY FATHER rented a house within walking distance of the high school, the shopping center, and the Kliment house. Princeton was a good walking town, its sidewalks lined with old sycamore trees. Walking distance to shopping was important, since there wasn't enough money for a car. My mother and brother walked to the shopping center, I walked to school, and my father had Mrs. Kliment's old Impala on loan so he could get to work. That was okay, though, because now we had a place to live.

The house was a pale green ranch with avocado green carpeting inside, beige plaid sofas, scarred wooden furniture throughout, and a basic kitchen. It came furnished, and a good thing too because you can't bring much in two suitcases for a family of four. I had my very own bedroom for the very first time. So did Patrik. Off the kitchen there was a dining room with an air conditioning in the window.

The bathroom had a toilet right next to the bathtub just like the Kliments had it, which made it sort of awkward, because, really. Suppose my dad had to pee while I was in the shower, right? Or suppose I had to do a stinky number two while my mom was in the bath? I tried my best to wrap my mind around all these little things in which the Americans were kind of… different. But this was the land of freedom, and I was eager to adapt. Perhaps, just like in Germany, body modesty wasn't that much of a big deal. If we had seen nude fathers and sons play soccer on a meadow by the Isaar River, with their dangly bits flopping all around, it only stood to reason that America would be even more free than that. Sharing bathrooms was, apparently, not that big of a deal.

The best part of the house, however, was the basement.

"There is a washing machine and a dryer, and they are right next to the sink!" My father rubbed his hands together, and his whole face glowed with excitement. "And there is a workbench, and there is a shelf right over the sink, where I can store my chemicals."

The three-bedroom furnished house was a fantastic deal, because with a bit of cunning, one could turn the basement into a chemical laboratory. You needed a few planks of wood to cover the washer and dryer for extra bench space. Cracking the window open provided adequate ventilation for most experiments. And *voilà*! You had space enough to create your own, American-dream chemical empire.

Beakers, graduated cylinders, Erlenmeyer flasks, a magnetic stirrer, and a thermometer joined a small digital scale, a proper laboratory notebook, and little bottles of various reagents on the shelves. All those things—and more—found their way into our basement, the first laboratory of S.K.Y. Polymers, Inc. Every day after my father came home from work at the Styrofoam factory, he disappeared into his basement lab.

My mother stood by the stove, working her dinner magic and wrestling with unfamiliar ingredients. My father was working his dinnertime magic downstairs, taming his exotic chemical reactions. Every so often his brown-haired head popped up from the basement.

"Do you have a spatula I could borrow?"

Mother handed him a clean spatula, unaware that she was giving it up for life. Spatulas, frying pans, and kitchen blenders: they all disappeared into the basement laboratory, never to be seen in the kitchen again.

"You can't use it now, it's contaminated," my father said.

"Why don't you buy your own blender, then?" my mother retorted.

"I didn't know I'd need a blender. We will go and buy you a new blender." And a new frying pan, and new spatulas, and new Pyrex measuring cups.

MY FATHER got off the telephone.

"Remember that guy, Josef, the pilot we met in Munich? He wants to come to America for a week and check it out. They aren't sure they want to settle in Germany."

My mother wrung a dishtowel in her hands, her feet apart as if for balance. She was standing her ground in her territory. Her slender frame psychically extended itself to the walls, her essence protecting kitchen appliances from the chemicals downstairs.

"When does he want to arrive?"

My parents weren't happy about Josef's visit. Maybe he was a spy, a double agent. Maybe he was going to find out something about us and carry the information back to the other side.

Eventually a decision had been reached to allow him in. He already knew where we lived; hiding was therefore useless. There was little to conceal. I was instructed to speak very little. My brother moved into my bedroom to make space for the unwanted guest.

Spring sprung sprightly that year and soon segued into temperatures I associated with swimming in muddy ponds. My mother, Patrik, and I were walking home from the Princeton Shopping Center, carrying groceries in European-style shopping bags.

Nobody else walked. They drove.

Father still drove Mrs. Kliment's Impala to work and back.

"We shouldn't have worried about our guest," my mother said. "He is too stupid to be a spy."

She was right. Josef the Pilot *loved* America. He loved the look, the feel of it. He loved the stores full of merchandise, with prices lower than those in Germany.

"So how much does the welfare office give you per month?" Josef asked after dinner, lingering over a glass of jug Chablis.

My father bristled. I saw his nostrils flare, and I leaned forward, eager for the fireworks.

"Well, first of all, Josef, we don't *need* any welfare. I have a job, and I am paid a decent salary. And secondly, the Americans don't give welfare to immigrants. You find a job, and you earn your way."

"You get nothing?" He was alarmed. Appalled, even. "How about this house? You pay the rent yourself?" His apartment in Germany was paid for by the German government, and his family received a welfare stipend from the Sozial-Amt. He was a military pilot, unqualified for other work. According to German law, he did not need to accept work either below or above his qualification level, *or* outside his field.

My father looked around, measuring the papered walls with his gaze. In Prague, we lived in Grandma and Grandpa's house where we had our own apartment on the third floor. My parents paid a nominal rent of 200 Kcs each month; my grandmother picked up the utilities. In America, adults and with children, my parents were on their own for the first time in their lives.

"Yep. Rent, utilities, telephone, food, clothing, all that. There are no great warehouses of free discards, like in Munich. We don't have any furniture yet—it comes with the house. But we will. The attitude here is different."

Josef's eyes were wide. "You mean you got nothing for free?"

"Sure we got some things for free," my mother interjected. "Our sponsors let us use one of their cars. And they spread the word, and all of their friends give us household items they don't need anymore. Blankets, kitchen pots, all those things you see around you."

"I got lunches for free for awhile," I volunteered. "In school. But I told the school I don't need them anymore since Dad's got a job."

The school secretary tried to talk me out of it, too. I didn't understand her reasoning since I didn't have my dictionary with me. I didn't want to be like the welfare kids in slow-track classes, using the red lunch tickets in the cafeteria. I wanted to be like the smart kids in regular classes who bought with cash.

Josef the Pilot stared into his glass for a long time. "That's it, then," he said. "We are staying in Germany.'

It was only two days later when my mother was preparing food in the kitchen that we heard commotion from the basement.

"Evacuate, evacuate, out of the house!" my father yelled from the basement. I heard the bifold metal basement doors creak open into the yard. An odd smell wafted up the basement stairs. I looked at my mother.

"Get out now!" she said forcefully. "I'll get Patrik."

We exited the house and walked around to the backyard. Josef the Pilot was already there, standing under the trees, peering across the sunbaked lawn into the dark maw of the open basement doors.

"Are you coming?" he called into the dark opening. My father ascended the short staircase, his laboratory notebook clutched in his arms, his eyes red from fumes. A red cloud of acrid smoke billowed out right behind him.

"Is there a fire?" My mother asked anxiously.

"No fire," my father said, gasping for breath.

"Shit, man, what the fuck happened, man? That was the weirdest fucking thing I've ever seen," Josef the Pilot said. Adrenaline was coursing though his veins, and the feeling of minor adrenaline levitation brought back the language of his military background.

We ignored him, staring at the thinning vapors wafting up the basement escape hatch.

"That only happened because you were talking at me," my father turned at him with accusation in his gaze. "I told you not to talk at me while I am mixing reagents." Contained anger barbed the edge of his voice.

He turned to my mother.

"I was doing another polymerization. I had my PAN in the beaker, all dissolved, and the last thing I had to add was phosphoric acid. Except, I was distracted by Josef here, talking at me. I grabbed the wrong bottle."

"What did you grab, dad?" I asked.

"Nitric acid." My father took a deep breath and shifted gears. From panic mode to teaching mode in one smooth exhale, he continued. "You see, nitric acid is much stronger than phosphoric, so the reaction proceeded a lot faster. And since polymerization is an exothermic reaction—it produces a lot of heat—and it happened fast, it sort of exploded."

"Exploded?" My mother honed in on the important word.

"Well not so much exploded as erupted, I guess. I was stirring the reagents and was watching it closely, and it's a good thing I had my eye on it despite Josef talking at me from the staircase, or else I might have missed the bubbles. Usually, you don't see bubbles, but I saw bubbles, and they were evolving faster and faster, and the mixture turned thicker and thicker, so I yelled, 'Get down!'" and we both hit the floor.

"Yeah, I know how to get down. It's in the training." Hitting the ground during an explosion was the only thing Josef the Pilot did right. He wanted us to notice.

"Yep, your chemist here, he sure got down right away! He hit the floor, belly and all. Immediately." It appeared our unwanted guest toned down his language, along with the slowly dissipating smoke. "And so did I! We were lucky—the contents of the beaker shot up and got stuck to the joists. Then this hot, acidic snot began to drip all over the place. And there was this nasty smoke—there's all kind of bad stuff in that, I bet."

My father and Josef the Pilot went on to theorize what vile chemicals might have been produced. They theorized for a long time, until the acidic snot-smoke could no longer be seen. My father got up and walked over to the red basement door, stuck his head over it, and gave it a sniff test.

"Not yet," he said.

We sat out there under the trees. The sun was beating down through the thin foliage and the cicadas were singing their hypnotic mating song. I felt the dry grass itch against my thighs, but there was nowhere else to go, and nothing else to do.

Every so often my father would go to the basement and the house, and check the air quality, hoping for a bit of breeze to stir the fumes through the open doors and windows.

Conversation began to lag.

Sweat ran down my nose. Its salt made me thirsty, and my mother chanced the acrid fumes for a quick trip inside for a pitcher of ice water and five glasses.

I started to really despise Josef the Pilot.

Five hours later, my father decided the house was probably safe. We left all the windows open till the next morning, just to make sure.

The basement survived pretty well. The acid-resistant pages of my father's laboratory notebook survived as well. His shirt and pants, decorated with acid holes, became his new work clothes. His calculator bore marks of the acid goo onslaught for years. I know, because he kept it even after better models came out.

Maybe it was the fear of being ejected from the house by an irate landlord, or maybe my mother put her foot down for the sake of general safety, but soon after the Josef eruption my father began to look around for a small laboratory space.

"NOW THAT we have start-up financing, I can open a lab," my father said happily few weeks later. His job at the Styrofoam factory wasn't going so well, but his hydrogel efforts were being well received. He produced plastics that could swell with amazing amounts of water, and unlike currently available products, they were strong at the same time. He fantasized about their potential uses. Better contact lenses; implants; medical devices; fish farming. This was foundational science, and the potential applications were as endless as human imagination.

"Don't quit your job yet," my mother said. They were drinking cheap jug wine after a group of investors left our dining room. I didn't understand all their words, but they spent a lot of time in the basement, and they all sat around the table and talked while the only air conditioner in the house blasted cold air.

I CAME from school to find my mother drunk. Patrik wasn't five years old yet. He sat in front of the television, his Matchbox cars and his plastic green soldiers on the floor before him. He lifted his eyes toward me with a confused and scared kind of a look.

"Hi, Mom," I said cautiously. I'd seen my mother drunk before, but other adults were around then, and they were drunk too. They were laughing and telling jokes, and that seemed okay somehow. Being home with my drunk mother and my little brother felt very different.

I felt very alone, and scared.

"All these entrepreneurs can go kiss my ass!" my mother yelled, wine almost spilling out of her glass. "They can just kiss my ass! We don't have nothing! People give us their cast-offs! If something happened to your father, how would we survive?"

She went on and on, her skinny butt pressed against the kitchen sink, her black hair plastered against her forehead in the heat of the day. Every so often she paused to take another sip of wine. Patrick peered around the corner tentatively, his eyes wide.

"Where is Dad?" he asked.

I BEGAN to dread coming home from school, afraid that my mother would be drunk again. She often was. Yet I hurried home quickly. I didn't know what might happen in my absence, and the responsibility for my little brother weighed heavily on my fourteen-year old shoulders.

The heat of late spring soaked into my shoulders and under my backpack, and the broad sycamore leaves provided just enough shade to make the walk home almost pleasant. The air conditioner would be on at home, blasting cold air over the dining room table, and the dark living room would feel cool and shady.

I burst through the door, looking forward to the cool relief.

There was no relief—the air was blasting, sure, but the house reeked of wine and cigarettes, and my mother was drunk in the sanctuary of her kitchen. She was draped over the sink with a glass in her hand.

She saw me walk in and turned toward me. The demanding shift of balance made her stumble—but it could have been her strappy, high-heeled sandals—and she opened her mouth.

Nothing good came out.

Just the same old fear, and hate, and more fear, tumbling out like murky miasma and threatening to stick to my skin. I backed away from her.

"Fucking communist pigs! But here it's no better! I never wanted come here, to a village such as this one!"

I eased my way into the living room. Patrik was sitting on the floor by the television, just like before, with his green soldiers forming his honor guard.

"How long has she been like this?" I hissed in his direction, trying to keep my voice low.

He shrugged. "A while. I don't know. Where's Dad?"

"At work." I looked up to see our mother lurch toward the dining room table, breaking her fall with her elbows against the Formica top.

"C-can you call him?"

"Let's see if she settles down," I said, keeping one eye on her, the other on my brother. He was almost five. Next year he'd go to kindergarten, away from the toxic fog that overtook our mother's rational faculties almost every afternoon.

Yet she didn't settle down, and just when I was contemplating taking Patrik to the shopping center or somewhere else—anywhere, really—he came up closer to me and put his hand on my arm.

Our family didn't hug much. His gesture caught my attention, and I looked in his eyes. He blinked twice before he pinned me with a determined gaze. "We really should call Dad."

I picked up the telephone. Calling my father at work felt like a dereliction of duty. I'd failed—once again—at controlling my mother's behavior.

"Who're you callin'?" Our mother stumbled toward me with a fierce expression.

"I'm calling Dad." As I said that, Patrick strategically relocated himself from the place in front of me to a position slightly behind me. I wished I could have done the same.

"Don't call him," she hiccupped. "Don't call that sonovabitch. He's the one brought us here to start with, an' I never wanted to come. Not this far, but nobody asked me. Me! Nobody asked me…" Keeping focus on the handwritten number was hard as she dissolved into blubbery tears almost within an arm's reach.

"Nobody asked me, but I'm going. I'm fucking going, and he can shove his stupid hydrogels up his ass!"

Her screech was interrupted by a female voice at the other side. I cupped my hand around the receiver to keep the noise out.

"May I speak to Dr. Stoy, please?"

He came on the line almost immediately. "What? Well, what is it?" He sounded impatient, secretive. Receiving personal calls at work was a sensitive matter.

"Dad… Mother is drunk again. I don't know what to do."

"What do you mean, 'again'?"

"Well, she has been doing this a lot, but usually she is quiet. Now she's yelling, though. I don't know how to make her stop." I heard his silence over the telephone wires.

"I'll see if I can come a little early," he said. "Hang in there. Take care of Patrick."

FATHER TALKED to Mother the next day. He made sure to spend more time with her, and I guess he spoke with the other Czech people who lived in the area, because we began to receive invitations to go places.

"Would you like to join me for yoga? It's a new form of exercise," said Mrs. Kliment. Mother did, once.

"Berlitz called me. They need somebody to teach this American diplomat to speak basic Czech, and they need it fast," Mrs. Kliment said. "I'd do it, but I have other things going on right now. Would you be interested? It's easy; you just speak Czech at him like he's a little child. The money's not great, but it's still money."

And thus, my mother set out every other day, leaving Mrs. Kliment to watch Patrik, who operated under strict orders to not destroy any more of Mr. Kliment's prized model airplanes.

It was exhausting work, but exhilarating. It held prestige. It paid a bit of money. We listened to her war stories over dinner, and enjoyed them.

Then the diplomat, with his hard-earned command of rudimentary Czech, left for his post.

"Can I say hello to anyone for you?" he asked her, brimming with gratitude.

"No! No. Please don't tell anyone my name." There was no telling how an innocent action, such as teaching a language to a diplomat, would affect the government's attitude toward our family in Prague.

"I CAN'T BE coming home early like this," my father said. "You just have to find a way to control her."

The idea of controlling my mother terrified me.

"Then at least make sure she doesn't injure herself. And take care of Patrik."

I was already doing that.

"I poured the wine out," he said. "It should be better this week."

It wasn't. Mother used the grocery money, bought more wine, and got entirely trashed. I spent the hours between school's end and my father's arrival watching her, running interference. She was surprisingly strong for a woman her size, and surprisingly loud.

"I am totally isolated here!" she sobbed. "There is nobody but Patrik! What am I supposed to do? I go to English classes at night, twice a week, but it's no good! Everybody there's an idiot! I don't want to be like that old Italian man! He's been here for forty years and I already speak better than he does!"

"Your English is fine, Mom," I said. "And next year, when Patrick's in school, you can start going to work, and you won't be isolated anymore."

"Work! I already do work! If I went to work who would cook? Who would take care of the family?" She poured herself some more wine.

"I could help," I offered.

"You!" she burst with derision. "You can't even do your own laundry!"

"Only because you won't let me!" I retorted. It was so unfair. I helped clean the house every Saturday. I scrubbed the bathroom and Windexed the inside and outside of all the windows. I put my clean clothes away. I dusted. My father vacuumed, his traditional role thus being fulfilled. If I could only make the bathrooms and windows sparkle clean enough, then maybe she wouldn't drink.

"I could cook," I offered tentatively.

"You can't even boil an egg."

Now that was perhaps true, but how would I ever learn if I was never allowed in the kitchen?

"I am isolated, and alone, and nobody here will help me!" she sobbed. "I am going back! I am going back to Prague!" I saw my mother peel her behind away from the kitchen sink and navigate her way out the front door in sudden, jerky movements. Mindful of how strong she could be, I carefully tried to stop her.

"No! You won't stop me! You all, all of you just try to control me!" she shrieked, pushed me aside, and wove out the door toward the hot sidewalk. Her high-heeled shoes impeded her progress and I wondered, idly, whether she would fall, and if she did, whether I would feel good about it.

I picked up the telephone and dialed a number from memory.

"I told you not to call me at work," my father hissed, his volume low. Work wasn't going all that well. The people he worked with wouldn't take his good advice because they couldn't allow a new immigrant with a thick foreign accent upstage their technological acumen.

"Dad, Mom is running away. Back to Prague. She is headed down Jefferson Road toward Valley Road. I think she lost a shoe. And she is yelling."

"I'll be right there." His voice was distant, resigned.

I felt like an utter failure. If my father lost his job because I couldn't control my mother's drinking, it would be my fault. And then we would be deported back to Czechoslovakia, because the Americans wanted only good immigrants, not depressed drunks. Nothing was worse than being deported. All that would be my fault too.

    I went to clean the bathroom again.

Chapter 9

TO PLUCK A DUCK

September 19th, 1980, Jefferson Road, Princeton, New Jersey, USA

THE AUTUMN of 1980 saw us in the same house my father rented last spring. After the explosion in the basement, my mother made him rent a separate laboratory, too. He still worked at a big chemical factory nearby. The job allowed him to finance both our family life and his entrepreneurial ambitions.

One of his co-workers, John, was a man who hunted. Hunting was a rare privilege in Czechoslovakia—it was one of those pseudo-aristocratic pastimes reserved for eligible Communist Party members and their cronies—but regular people rarely saw a firearm outside of their compulsory military service. Knowing a regular, flesh-and-blood person who actually dressed in green, grabbed a gun and headed for the woods felt foreign and exotic. This was, after all, America. A land where the frontier was still tangible and vast. Whole states sat almost empty, full of forests or huge agricultural fields. Their population was miniscule compared to New York City or Philadelphia or Washington. They still had Indians, which were rare on the ground in Princeton. When I inhaled, I could feel how free the air was, and how far it stretched. It was clean and endless and exotic compared to the staid, overpopulated Europe.

In America, you didn't feel layers upon layers of dead ancestors piled under your feet. Hundreds and thousands of years worth of tribes and invaders and nations. The first sculptors of fertility statues, the makers of La Tene pottery, the Celts vanquished by the Slavs who braved the forested mountains north of the country and found a land that was "empty" and yet full of the "milk and honey" that took settled people to raise. Then the Premyslids and Germanic traders and Mongol invaders. Dynasties clad in chain mail and steel, builders of castles and churches and fish farming ponds. Graveyards in Europe filled to overflowing with ancient bones—so full, so old, so common—that they had to be dug up every so often and deposited in grotesque patterns in ossuaries. In the old country, all those layers of long-dead ancestors were always there looking over your shoulder, having breathed the air you were now breathing and having eaten the same rye bread you had for breakfast every morning. Their ghosts pushed and crowded around you, nosy and curious.

We left them all in Europe.

In America, there was enough room to spread your arms wide. The Indian ghosts did not bother us, for they were not our kin. Air fragrant with the foreign honeysuckle gave way to the smell of late-season barbecues. There was enough air to breathe, enough space to stretch your dreams. Apparently, enough space to hunt, too.

DURING this exceptionally hot autumn, when I wished the municipal pool was still open, my father came home one evening with a curiously excited expression. After some ceremony, he produced a paper bag and handed it to my mother with all due reverence.

"Here. John got back from a hunting trip and he's sent us a duck."

My mother pulled the dead, feathered bird out of his bag and eyed the carcass with a dubious eye.

"That's nice. But who will do the plucking?"

"Oh don't worry, I'll pluck it," my father said. His eyes gleamed with excitement and his face was flushed, aglow with that uplifted, adventurous expression he used to get before we went fish poaching. He'd always had that glow about him when a piece of game meat was around.

"But this duck isn't like the other ducks," my mother objected. "Other ducks come from the store, they are plucked and cleaned and gutted. I don't know the first thing about plucking a duck, and besides, didn't you say he shot it? There will be bits of lead in the meat and we'll just break our teeth!"

My father remained undaunted.

"Indeed, you are correct! This duck is like no ordinary duck. It's better! It's better because it came from the wild. It will have an extraordinary, wild taste. I've read about it in books." He paused, retrieving data. "All the books say you have to let game meat age. You have to hang it."

He wiped the sweat off his brow.

"I still think you should throw it out." My mother looked at the dead fowl as though it was a biohazard.

"But Mom," I chimed in. "Suppose I pluck it. How often do you get to eat a real, wild duck?"

"If you pluck it, I'll roast it," she agreed after a pause. "But I'm not touching the feathers. It looks like a pain in the butt."

It *was* a pain in the butt. The feathers were firmly embedded in the duck's skin and hand no intention of parting ways with their natural home. I yanked as hard as I could, unaware that the bird should have been scalded in hot water to loosen the massive feather follicles—and apparently the books didn't refer to this minor step either, because my father's solution was to hand me a pair of pliers.

"Just grab the feathers and yank. Like this, see?" He grasped two feathers at a time in the teeth of the pliers and gave a hard yank. Success! The bird was two feathers short.

It took me an hour to clear a patch the size of my palm. The duck skin was nothing like the white, pink-tinged skin of a store-bought bird.

The skin was purple.

"Dad, check this out! What do you think is wrong with this duck?"

"Lemme see… nothing 's wrong! It's just a bruise."

"A bruise?"

"Sure! It was up in the air when it was shot, and it fell to the ground. It got bruised upon impact. That's totally normal."

My mother's remark regarding the pooling of blood was summarily disregarded.

"Maybe the duck will be easier to pluck once the meat has aged a bit," my father opined, eyeing the dead, partially exfoliated bird with the expert eye of a champion duck connoisseur. I was only too eager to agree – anything was an excuse enough to stop plucking. My hands ached from the unaccustomed effort. After all, if the meat aging theory held, the plucking would get easier in a few days.

MY FATHER was an engineer in both attitude and training, and as such, he determined that the most practical place to hang the duck was in the shady breezeway that connected the house with the garage. The poor bird hung there by the neck like a convicted felon, a lifeless sentinel who greeted all that had the temerity to approach our front door.

"The bird can't stay here. It looks… disturbing." My mother's assessment of the situation only pointed to the fact that she didn't want to break a tooth on lead shot. She was adventurous enough to fish for trout, gut the fish, and fry it up, even if it meant poaching and incurring the wrath of the local fish warden. She hiked through the woods, foraged for wild mushrooms, and even ate them. She wasn't a complete stranger to adventure, But she drew her line at the fowl corpse that swayed in the breeze. His feathers —it had been a male—still had that lovely sheen and brilliant colors. I walked up and stroked the multi-hued wings. They were so exotic. If I was a real Indian I'd want them in my headdress.

My mother must have read my thoughts. "I wouldn't put those feathers in your hair. They probably have bugs in them." Then she turned to my father. "Move it somewhere else."

The easiest solutions are the best. My father placed the deceased duck on the ping-pong table in the stand-alone garage. It lay there on the corner, and I didn't really mind because it was too hot to play ping-pong anyway.

"It better not start smelling," my mother said.

"The books say a duck should age for a week," my father said. Then he turned toward me. "In the meanwhile, maybe you could finish plucking it. Just a bit every day, and before you know it, the bird will be done!"

I nodded, but my assent came with great hesitation. I might have been barely fifteen, but even I knew that meat decays over time, and the higher the temperature, the faster it will go. I plucked a bit of the duck the first day, and a bit more the second day. On the third day, the bird began to bloat. I wrinkled my nose at the foreign smell filling the garage.

"I don't know, Mom," I said. "Do you think this will actually be safe to eat?"

My mother looked over my shoulder and crinkled her nose. "Ugh. Your father better finish plucking it soon, or I'm throwing it in the garbage."

THE NEXT day was a mail day. My grandmother tried to mail us two kilograms of Czech books every week, taking advantage of a special book rate. She was determined to mail my parents their whole library. We all knew the mailman by then, and he was kind enough not to leave the shipments out in the open, where they might be stolen.

That week, my mother was coming back from a shopping trip with my little brother in tow. She walked up the driveway with a bag in each hand just as the mailman stumbled out the side door of the garage. He was pale in the face and gasping for breath.

"I… I got a package for you," he rasped, and then he gulped in more hot autumn air.

"Thank you," my mother smiled. "You look hot. Would you like some water?"

He only nodded. It was a while before he stumbled back down the road.

MY FATHER came home at five-thirty, when the heat of the day was still near its peak. As soon as he set his briefcase down, my mother issued her ultimatum.

"You have to finish plucking the duck tonight, and I'm baking it tonight. Or, even better, just throw it out!"

"Oh, I'll do it. Don't worry." He gave her a concerned smile. "What's wrong?"

"The mailman left us another package of books from my mother," she said. "He always puts them on the ping-pong table. When he walked into that hot garage, the smell of the duck must have hit him right in the face! I have never been so embarrassed. It's a good thing I found out only after he left. What must he think of us?"

I didn't know the proper English word for the smell that assaulted my senses when I followed my father into the garage. Today I'd call it "decomp."

"Dad, are you sure it's safe to eat?" I asked. I didn't like the idea of touching the vile bird, let alone eating it.

"Sure it is! It's just aging. The more aged it is, the better it is! The books say it should age for a week, and it's been only three days…" He leaned against the doorjamb, considering the matter from afar. "A typical chemical reaction doubles in rate every ten degrees Centigrade. It's been pretty warm… I guess it's aged enough!" He slid a hopeful, exploratory glance in my direction. "Shall we pluck?"

I shook my head. I didn't refuse to do anything my parents asked of me on general principle, but touching a smelly, decomposing carcass was rather removed from my comfort zone.

"I think you should do it. Your hands are so much stronger."

He nodded. "Stronger. Hm." He didn't look fooled by my rationale, but he did set up shop on the stoop of the back kitchen door, and in half an hour, the bird was bare.

"It's amazing how much easier the feathers come out when you let the bird age a bit!" His comment had that lemons-into-lemonade feel to it, though, and my mother must have thought so as well.

"How about you remove the guts, then, and I'll pre-heat the oven. And I'll put up hot dogs, just in case."

"Just in case what?" he grumbled, but he did put the plucked duck onto a cutting board and slid a sharp knife up its anus. "You have to make a cut from the butt up to the breastbone," he said. "Although I'm surprised John didn't do this part already. I seem to recall the books saying something about disemboweling the bird right away." A cloud of dark premonition passed across his brow, followed by the most revolting stench I'd ever experienced.

I almost gagged.

"Dad, that smells terrible!"

"Yeah. Come to think of it, I seem to recall reading that the guts should be removed right away. I wonder why John hadn't done that." My father's face had a look of grim determination now. I backed out the kitchen door and slumped on a garden wall in the shade, where my mother joined me. She lit up a cigarette.

"I don't know how we'll be eating that," she said. "I'll roast it, but I'm just making potatoes to go with it. There's no use wasting time and making dumplings. I bet even he won't eat it."

"I'll eat it!" My father had apparently overheard her. "It will be nice and gamy. Just you wait!"

THE ODOR of this particular roasting duck was nothing like the ones I'd smelled before. My mother and I exchanged meaningful looks, while my brother scampered around with the obliviousness of a five-year-old. His focus was on his plastic green soldiers, and on the upcoming promise of hot dogs.

I set the table. My mother brought out a bowl of boiled potatoes, and heated-up sauerkraut from the can.

The potatoes looked like food, safe to eat.

The sauerkraut emanated the fresh and tart happiness that brought well-roasted food to mind.

Then she brought out a roasting pan with the star of the show: the mutilated, mostly-plucked carcass of a wild-caught waterfowl, aged according to a book my father had read many years ago.

"Here, why don't you carve it," my mother said as she pushed the fork and sharp kitchen knife toward my father.

He took a deep breath. That was probably a mistake, judging from the face he made.

"Okay," he said. "I'll carve it."

And he did. He sliced the breast and separated the legs and the wings. Usually, the thigh was a choice cut and we bickered over it. "Who wants the thigh?" he asked.

A resounding silence was his reply.

"Well, then. I will eat the leg." His face contorted with stubborn determination. "This will be nice and gamey. It came from the wild." He gesticulated with the unfortunate, roasted limb. "The wild!"

We all allowed him to serve us a very small piece, because we didn't want to hurt his feelings. Our plates were loaded up with sauerkraut and potatoes and a very small piece of duck breast, and in my brother's case, an Oscar Meyer wiener.

We sat in silence for a short while, but it wasn't the respectful sort of silence that some religious people do over their meals. It was more like a staring contest, wherein we waited for someone else to be the guinea pig. My father broke the impasse.

"Enjoy the meal," he said, uttering the familiar Czech phrase.

"Enjoy the meal," we all murmured back.

We remained still. Our hands were poised over our silverware, wanting to get the ordeal over with but not quite willing to do the deed itself. It reminded me of the time when my cousins and I dared one another to touch an electrified cow fence.

Rising to his responsibility as the leader of our pack, my father cleared his throat. He cut off a piece of the glistening, brown leg meat, piled a lot of sauerkraut onto it, and ate it.

We watched him closely.

He chewed, breathing through his wide-open nostrils. His eyes had a wide, focused look, the kind I associated with my little brother making an especially hard BM on the potty only three years ago. After more chewing, he swallowed.

"Yep, it's pretty gamey," he said. "It's edible, though."

The rest of us cut a small bundle of muscle fibers and put it in our respective mouths.

My brother, apparently eager for his hot dog, spat it out right away. My mother, a diplomatic woman, kept rolling it around her mouth, until she finally chased it with a solid forkful of sauerkraut, and swallowed.

"I am sorry but I don't think this is good anymore," she said.

I really wanted the duck to work out. I tried and tried, but it was hard to get past the taste of charred decomp in my mouth. The duck was shot in the wild with a real gun, American-style, plucked in alternating bursts of benign neglect, and aged under alarming temperatures.

I tried to like it, I really did, but that little piece was all I could swallow before joining my little brother in his hot dog orgy.

My father sat at the head of the table as though carved from stone. Only his hands moved, his hands and his jaw. His breathing was shallow, presumably so that he didn't have to smell any more of his dinner than he absolutely had to.

"You don't have to finish," my mother cajoled him. "No sense getting sick over a duck!"

"There's nothing wrong with this duck," he said. "It's maybe a bit gamey, that's all." He was a man on a mission, determined to enjoy a wild-hunted duck that was a gift and that was aged to perfection. Once he finished eating what was on his plate, he pushed it away. "Well, maybe it was a bit too gamey," he allowed. Then he poured himself a stiff whiskey.

My mother disposed of the duck under the cover of darkness. Only a pile of lead shot was left by the kitchen sink.

Chapter 10

FRESHLY KILLED FISH

December 24th, 1980, Deer Creek Drive, Princeton, New Jersey, USA

CHRISTMAS EVE had always been a day of pandemonium back in Prague, and our first Christmas in Princeton wasn't much different.

My parents fixed a Christmas tree in its stand first thing in the morning. There seemed to have been something wrong with it, though, because its branches were thickly packed together.

"There's no space for the candles," my mother said with some concern. She'd managed to procure Victorian-era candles and tree candleholders, yet the tree seemed curiously ill suited to accepting them.

"The Kliments say people here use electrical lights," my father said.

We all grimaced. Electrical lights! How tasteless. How fake. And probably unsafe, what with people tripping over cords, and every spark from every short circuit waiting to ignite the evergreen torch while we were asleep. Candles were familiar and probably a lot safer to boot.

"Maybe we could weigh the branches down, train them to open up a bit," my mother said.

All day long, the tree stood in the middle of the living room like a piece of bizarre modern art. Its bushy branches supported heavy pots and pans. Meat cleavers and mallets hung pendulously like clumsy ornaments of a homicidal giant—all in an effort to help the stubborn, bushy branches relax and open up enough to safely accept lit candles.

After many hours of being unable to cook with her most commonly used kitchen implements, and not realizing much success in training the stubborn American Christmas tree, my mother strategically pruned some of the extra branches out, trimming the tree to her specifications. Hanging ornaments had always been her job in Prague, one that she jealously guarded from well-meaning yet clumsy volunteers. She enjoyed it and she was good at it. The tree had to be perfect, worthy of opening the gifts deposited under it.

In America, most people open their gifts on Christmas morning. This makes good sense, for it allows the parents some slack to get in position to perform their appointed tasks. Our family was willing to Americanize, but we weren't willing to change the deeply ingrained ritual of opening gifts after dinner, and furthermore, we were confused by new schedules and customs.

And what was this talk of Santa Claus, anyway? Everybody knows that St. Nicholas came on his feast day, November 6th, and brought children fruit, nuts, and maybe a bit of candy. Coal, too, if they were naughty. He had no need to show up on Christmas when his job was already done.

Christmas was the time Baby Jesus would magically deposit gifts under the tree while the family enjoyed their silent Christmas dinner. Silent, because we always ate fish, and if you speak while eating fish, you'll end up getting a needle-bone stuck in your throat. The way my parents talked about things, stray fish bones were a lot more dangerous than live candles on the Christmas tree.

BACK IN PRAGUE, the season usually started with early St. Nicholas sightings.

"I saw St. Nicholas doing his rounds on my way home," my grandfather would always utter as though by sheer coincidence. He said this to my grandmother, not to me. He lifted his formidable eyebrow, conveying grave significance. Then he turned his attention to me.

"I wonder if he will stop at our house this year. I wonder if you were good enough?"

I wondered too. Maybe he would skip. Or worse, maybe he'd come escorted by the Devil, and the Devil would take his belt and whip my butt for having been naughty, talking back, and not putting my toys away. Some kids said it had happened to them.

After dinner on November 6th, we'd all hear a knock on the main house door and my parents would run all seven flights downstairs to open it. I'd hear the voice of Saint Nicholas, asking for me.

"Come in, come in! Welcome to our house. The children are waiting upstairs. We hope they haven't been very bad this year."

I stood waiting, dreadful anticipation freezing me in the far corner of the kitchen, not knowing whether he would be escorted by the Devil or not. Every year, I hoped with all my heart that he'd come and bring an Angel if I was especially worthy.

His tall frame filled the doorframe, dressed in a white robe with a white tabard bearing gold crosses on the front and the back. A tall, white bishop's mitre sat on his head, decorated with gold crosses like a royal crown.

He bore a shepherd's crook, and some said he was known to discipline unruly children with it. He had unmistakable white hair, a white beard, white eyebrows, and a deep voice, and it didn't do you any good to look him in the eye too much. Which is why my brother Patrik had noticed, when he had been only three years old: "Look, St. Nicholas has the same shoes as my grandpa!"

He asked whether we were good or bad, and wanted to know what naughty things we did. And this was good, because I got to confess to all the pieces of property I'd broken, vandalized, or otherwise defaced during the year. I'd fess up to lying, to letting my friend copy off my math test, and to stealing raisins from the pantry even though I knew Grandma had to go from store to store in search of them. I had always been forgiven by Saint Nicholas, which was great, because my parents had to look on in amazement and couldn't do a thing about it.

It was amnesty time.

After he admonished me to try harder to be good, Saint Nicholas deposited a basket on the floor, instructed me to enjoy it, but to keep all the chocolate, foil-covered figurines for Christmas. I eyed the fresh oranges and apples with appreciation because they weren't canned. Dates thrilled me especially, because they were sweet. In that sweetness I could taste the essence of places that were exotic and far away.

WE WERE in America now, and even though I was too old for a personal Saint Nicholas visitation, my brother was still just the right age. Except here, a whole ocean away, Saint Nicholas didn't make personal visits and offer amnesty for broken vases or snitched and eaten raisins. The tradition didn't belong. I steeled my heart against grief that I wasn't allowed to feel. We were all in it together, and bringing up old things and idle wishes would have only burdened the rest of the family.

I sucked it up, knowing I'd never again dress up as an angel with white hair made of cotton, with carefully cut out paper wings pinned to my back. I'd never again wear my mother's old ball gown to visit the little kids next door, be their Angel, and feel like I was "in on it."

Instead, Santa Claus had it all organized and automated, dropping gifts down chimneys from his supersonic reindeer-driven sleigh while servicing the whole continent in one night. It was a big-time operation. It was so very American.

BACK IN PRAGUE, Grandma always began her cookie baking on St. Nicholas day. Varieties and flavors marched on in a steady and unchanging progression: anisettes, almond and coconut meringues, sandwich jelly cookies, nut rolls, nut and chocolate molds. Batches upon batches of Christmas cookies were stored in shoeboxes in grandma's linen closet, and if not there, then among her sewing supplies, or under her silk scarves, or behind grandpa's folded shirts. I ferreted out every hiding place.

They were so excellent. So rare. So good. The trick was not to take too many, and to rearrange the layers so that the pilfering wasn't obvious.

"You were after the cookies again," Grandma would say every so often. "I'm glad you like them, but we need them for Christmas. If we have guests, we need to offer them something special, and I can't make more. There are no more hazelnuts this year. I was lucky to get the little there was—and the line was almost two hours long."

Three days before Christmas, my mother and my grandmother and I would go to a small open-air market. The air normally smelled of coal smoke and decayed chestnut leaves, but on a fish market day there was also a whiff of far-away ponds in the breeze. A touch of mud, lots of water, fish slime and fresh entrails that hadn't begun to spoil tinted the air. Giant, wooden tubs of fish off-loaded from trucks were now seated on the weathered blacktop of a makeshift marketplace. They were big enough to swim in. The dark water within boiled with the glistening bodies of carp passing over and around one another in a never-ending dance.

I watched my mother and grandmother debate how big a fish, how many, which one. They pointed, and the fishmongers pulled the live carp out in a net, weighed them, and wrapped them in old newspapers. The more squeamish customers, those who knew nothing of proper cooking, had their fish killed and gutted. For us, though, having live fish was the only way and, being carp and virtually indestructible, they always survived the half-hour walk home.

When we arrived the bathtub was already filled, waiting for the new guests. I spent hours perched on the rim of the tub, watching the fish, fascinated by their graceful movement and the slick slime covering their shimmering scales.

"You are not giving them names, are you?" my mother asked, concerned. "Once you name an animal, it's harder to eat it."

"Mom, can't we keep at least one? They're so beautiful."

"And where would we keep them?" The corners of her mouth pulled up in a smile.

"We would dig a little pond in the lawn. And we could swim in it in the summer, too."

"Like we could keep a horse in the garage?" she said, replaying her own childhood dreams, which strangely coincided with mine.

"Yeah." We observed the hypnotic movement of the fish in silence.

"Mom, how about a fish tank? Just a little one." I tried to parlay my fascination with carp into a fish tank every year.

"No. Too much trouble, and your fish will all die."

THE YEAR before we left she'd expanded on the standard reply.

"Do you remember the time we watched that pond at Třeboň being fished out, when you were three? You were such a cute child. Everyone gave you things. And this old grizzled fisherman—nobody would have guessed he'd notice a little girl—he picked the biggest fish and gave it to you. Put it right in your arms."

I remembered. The fish felt heavy and tried to breathe air. It didn't belong in my arms. It didn't belong in the net, nor in those large tubs.

"And then you looked at him, looked at the fish, looked at him, looked at the fish, and then you marched down to the edge of the pond and put it back in the water. And he was so mad I thought he would say something, but he didn't."

The fish had belonged in the water.

But I never felt sorry for the carp in our bathtub. I never minded watching my father kill them, breaking their thick spine with an ax in my grandmother's kitchen. The rose and maroon entrails oozed from the cavities of their freshly killed bodies. My grandmother removed them, careful not to rupture the gall bladder. She let me cajole her into extracting the double air bladder. It was like a slick balloon, floating in a bowl of water until rougher play punctured it.

When the killing and the gutting was over, my mother reentered the kitchen and helped scale the fish. Large, glistening, coin-like scales flew all over, stubbornly sticking to the table, floors, chairs, and walls.

"Put one in your purse, it will attract money," my grandfather said. That's how it was done in the village when he was growing up.

"If only you'd help instead of talking nonsense, old man," my grandmother spouted. "Get out of the kitchen! You're in the way."

My grandmother breaded the fish for frying, while my mother set out to make soup from the heads and the skeletons and then finish decorating the potato salad.

The potato salad, a visual centerpiece of the table, had always been my mother's specialty. It contained ham and potatoes and pickles and cooked carrots and celery root and God only knows what else, all bound together with yellow mayonnaise. She smoothed its surface with a spatula, applying a thin coating of mayonnaise like a painter applies gesso to the canvas. Then she set out to create.

Cooked carrot slices were cut into fanciful shapes with jelly cutters; pickles were sliced and cut to make palm leaves; boiled eggs were decorated with anchovy paste and capers—every year, she added something new and fresh and interesting. Red pickled peppers, capers, out-of-season parsley. We were not allowed to help, or even to comment. Our job was to admire her creation, which we did. I couldn't wait until I was old enough to decorate a potato salad too.

And that very day, on top of all the killing and cooking, the tree had to go up in a separate room. Once I grew old enough not to believe in supernatural gifts, I was allowed to help my parents set up the tree. My father made it stand straight by tying it to tall furniture. My mother was the decorating expert:

First the heavy chocolates.

Then the candles in their clip-on holders.

Then, heaven bless, more chocolates wrapped in foil.

Then the glass ornaments, going from the largest to the smallest.

Then the sparklers, the explosive-dipped wire positioned away from tree needles to prevent a fire.

And finally, a last touch, some thin gold chains and tinsel, always positioned to avoid the candles, and always reevaluating whether the branch supporting each candle was sturdy, straight, and free of obstructions that could turn the celebration of Eternal Light into one glorious blaze.

Meanwhile, Grandpa set the table in another room. Christmas Eve being a fasting day devoid of lunch, we always looked forward to a silent dinner.

Silence for the Christmas dinner not only honored the concept of "Christmas Peace," it was also a medical necessity. Everybody ate fried carp, and carp has wicked sharp bones that will lodge in the throat at the slightest provocation. Emergency rooms were full of unfortunate carp eaters every year, and every year, one of us had a close call. There was nothing more embarrassing than breaking the Christmas Peace by doing a cat-passing-a-hairball impersonation at the table.

First you'd put a small piece of fish in your mouth. Then you'd press it against the palate with your tongue and move it around. This action revealed any needle bones that might have been missed in the kitchen. If you found a bone, you'd put it at the edge of your plate. Only then you'd swallow—and only then you could ask Mom to pass the potato salad. So we would sit there and eat, very silent to keep the sharp fish bones out of our throats, and also to hear the little tinkling bell from the

Christmas tree, which indicated when a divine visitation took place.

For us kids, the dinner seemed to drag on forever. There was the obligatory fish soup with croutons. Then the delicious but potentially lethal carp, which had to be eaten slowly, accompanied by the special potato salad. For dessert, we had a compote, a bounty of garden fruit which my grandmother canned so conscientiously. Apricots, pears, gooseberries and currants floated in their juices, nestled in a smoky grey, cut-crystal bowl.

"That bowl is from the First Republic, so don't break it," my grandmother reminded us, careful to protect her wedding gifts from better days. "They don't make them like that anymore."

When the long-awaited bell split the silence, we turned off all the lights and went to the room where my Uncle Slavek used to sleep. The tree's glory dominated a universe that was cloaked in darkness except for the candlelit branches, and the sparklers ejecting constellations with a gentle hiss. My grandfather sat at the piano and played old Christmas carols and we sang while the stars shooting from the sparklers reflected in the glass globes, and the candles dripped hot wax onto the resin-saturated needles.

"We should put those candles out," one of the adults would say nervously as whole minutes of live fire hazard ticked off, one by one.

"Don't worry, there is a bucket of water over by the coal stove," my grandmother would inevitably reply as she eyed the glowing tree with fondness in her one good eye.

The sparklers burned themselves out. Someone flicked on a light switch, and the incandescent glow banished the ancient magic for another year, back into the shadows of elder days.

Our gifts were wrapped in recycled, reused wrapping paper saved from many Christmases in a row. There were several gifts for each person. I always got a stack of books, a new sweater, and at least one cool thing to play with. Christmas carols played on the radio and the smell of frankincense and myrrh still lingered in the air as we settled down with our books over a generous tray of Christmas cookies.

Here in America, my mother set out to replicate our traditional Czech Christmas. She found it to be a gargantuan, if not impossible, task.

"They don't have live carp anywhere," she said. "Apparently, Americans don't eat carp at Christmas."

In fact they would think keeping three large fish in your bathtub like we did in Prague as somewhat eccentric. Americans didn't know how to have a good time.

"That's a shame." I would miss seeing the carp swim to and fro, their graceful tails swishing from side to side, their full, firm lips opening and closing in a silent symphony with the movement of their gills. I would miss seeing my father chop their heads off with an ax, and watching my mother and my grandmother scale them, with smelly, fishy scales flying all over the kitchen.

"Remember that huge carp you let go when you were three?" My mother eyed me wistfully. "We sure could use that carp right now."

My parents chickened out on the candle issue.

"It's a rented house. Imagine if we burned it down. We might get evicted. We might even get deported!"

We lit the tree with electrical bulbs and hung ornaments bought in K-Mart. Then we cooked and cleaned and enjoyed some of my mother's Christmas cookies. I'd never realized how much work goes into Christmas. Now that we were on our own, I was not only allowed to step into the kitchen, but my help was even appreciated. I was, for the first time in my life, allowed to handle food. Nothing critical, mind you.

"Here, slice these pickles for me," my mother would say while making the fish soup. "No, not like that—like *this*."

There was a lot to do. Patrik and I set the table. Dad vacuumed. We all offered help, but Christmas had to be perfect and nobody can do it as well as Mom, so… our imperfect efforts were often deemed to cause more harm than good. We were allowed to glue the jam cookies together, if not to give them their final dusting of powdered sugar.

At six-thirty, dinner was served.

"This fish isn't the same," my mother complained. "It tastes different."

My father nodded in agreement. "It's still good, though. You did a great job."

"And the cookies! I don't have the right cookie cutters. The flour is different here, too."

All that effort and pain and fatigue, and the Christmas dinner still wasn't perfect. Because it wasn't the same.

We opened our numerous gifts. There was a lot of clothing, and house-wares, and power tools, and toys. My brother was in school now and was learning how to read and write. His teachers informed him that his name wasn't "Patrik," but "Patrick." He picked up the extra consonant in an effort to fit in, and since he liked his new name, we didn't complain.

For the first time, his Christmas gifts were labeled for "Patrick." Good thing his name was easy. At least he wasn't named after Mom's father. "Bohuslav" translated as "Glory of God," and I snickered at the thought of the teachers trying to standardize *that.*

"We should call home again."

"The lines might still be busy."

It took three more tries to get through. Grandma and Grandpa on the other side sounded a world away, their voices chased by that odd, trans-oceanic echo the old-fashioned transoceanic cables used to make. Yes, they made fish and salad, and they had a small tree. Yes, Grandma baked some cookies. Not as many as when we were there—there was no point in it. Yes, they'd received our letter and our gifts. The gifts had arrived opened, and the letters reviewed by the police, but most of it seemed to be there. We wished one another Merry Christmas carefully, aware of silent, institutional listeners recording our words.

"Did you know the mistletoe is different here?" my mother said to her mother. "Its berries are smaller, and the leaves are formed differently. It's not the same. Not as nice."

In America you could only buy sad, preserved, dye-enhanced little sprays of *Viscum americanum*, a poorer cousin of the *Viscum abum* that used to fill a large crystal vase back in Prague. Certainly no substitute for a plant full of power that was to bring the whole house luck for the year to come—and even had enough power to have killed an ancient god.

It wasn't even medicinal.

"Does that fit okay? It looks good on you."

"This is a great book. I love the drill bits."

"Can we hook up that video game now?"

"You didn't have to spend so much."

We made do without candles and carp, without myrrh and mistletoe. This was an American Christmas. The food was plentiful and the gifts were abundant. Even the Christmas tree was nice—you could leave it on all evening long, no buckets of water needed.

My parents sipped their wine at the table, their energy spent. Patrick shot skeet with a little ray gun on the television, and I put a record on my new stereo—it would stay in the living room for everyone to use, of course. What, was I crazy? Why would I want a stereo in my bedroom?

"This is not so bad," my father said.

"No, it turned out okay" my mother said. Her relief at it being over had overshadowed her misgivings over the lack of traditional things. There was over a foot of snow outside, and the Kliments were going to visit for a glass of wine and some cookies in a little bit.

People are adaptable. I didn't realize it at the time, but as soon as we put those electric lights on that tree, we had begun a transformation process that consisted of internal negotiations and compromises. We were adapting, and this American Christmas wasn't so bad after all. In fact, it was pretty darn good.

Chapter 11

FAMILIAL CLOSENESS

January 10th, 1981, Deer Creek Drive, Princeton, New Jersey, USA

"WE NEED to make more space," my mother said, surveying our rental house.

The large, heat-sucking windows were now draped in natural-color fabric. The four bedrooms would have to hold not four, but eight individuals. My father's brother, Uncle George, took his family out of Czechoslovakia one year after we defected. They were going to stay with us. My vision was filled with a memory of our idyllic cohabitation during summer vacations. It was going to be awesome.

"We will stay in the master bedroom, uncle and aunt can go next to us in Dad's office, Misha and Marketa can share Patrick's room, and Patrick can share your room." And thus it was done.

Our little Toyota Celica groaned under the weight of extra mattresses, bought used in a seedy Trenton second-hand store. Trenton neighborhoods also yielded reasonably priced carpet remnants. A flea market at Washington Crossing supplied us with varied, yet wonderful sterling silver eating utensils. They cost less than stainless would have at K-Mart. Pots and pans were acquired through the careful accumulation of Green Stamps, pasted into a green stamp book, and exchanged for kitchenware in a local supermarket. Once again, the Princeton Czech community and their friends scoured their houses and donated spare bedding and clothes.

"Mom, where's Dad?" I asked breathlessly as I jumped off my birthday bicycle.

"Cleaning his office."

I parked the bike in the carport and ran inside, ripping my jacket off, breathing on my red fingers to get them warm again. Whatever question I was going to ask my father had fluttered out of my mind as I entered the room which was his office, and which would now become Uncle George's and Aunt Vera's bedroom.

My father sat in his office chair facing the desk. On each side of his chair was a large, black garbage bag. He picked up a piece of paper, looked it over, pronounced a judgment of doom over it and tossed it, crumpled, into the garbage bag on his left side. He repeated the process several more times. Then a new paper caught his attention.

"Oh ho! Our car insurance! We need to hold onto that." And he carefully slid the document into the garbage bag on his right side. He continued clearing the pile on his desk, robot-like, for some minutes before he turned around.

"What are you doing, Dad?" I asked. The room looked chaotic with the furniture moved around, and the floor yet unswept. Dust bunnies still danced where Aunt Vera and Uncle George's mattresses would lie on the floor.

"I am clearing all of this out! And I have a scientific method. Look! One bag goes, the other bag stays." He was jazzed. He was working away, finally releasing the clutter that comes with wild bursts of imaginative work done on too little sleep.

I backed out slowly. My job was clear. Get my room ready for Patrick's mattress to be placed on the floor somewhere, and make space for his clothes and his toys. Little did we know that my father would accidentally throw out the bag with the important documents, and keep the bag with all the garbage. Birth certificates, passports, green cards, and credit card statements would all become new residents at some New Jersey landfill.

MY COUSINS' family arrived in the large Impala, once again borrowed, to accommodate more people and their luggage. Just like us, the new family of four brought very little with them.

The car pulled into the driveway, and Aunt Vera emerged first. She looked around, jet-lagged and bleary-eyed. Her auburn hair shone red in the wintry sun. My father and Uncle George got out and took care of the luggage while Aunt Vera rousted the kids out of the back seat.

"Wake up, we're here."

My cousins were both younger than I, but at least they were girls. Misha was close in age, barely two years my junior, and she seemed thin and pale and shy, not at all like the cheerful co-conspirator who had played cowboys and Indians and stole peas, poppy heads, and corn with me from the state-owned fields. Marketa was two years older than Patrick, her long blond hair spilling down over her thick-knit sweater. She smiled when she saw me, her cousin "Katka." Visiting family was always a grand adventure.

JUST LIKE ME, the girls hadn't attended school in Munich. Just like me, they were ushered to their respective school within days, dictionary in hand. Just like me, Misha skipped the whole eighth grade and entered in the middle of the ninth.

If Katka was intelligent enough to skip a grade and a half, then Misha was too.

"Misha is so nice and thin," my mother said, looking her over in my presence. What I heard her say was, "You still haven't lost any weight."

My weight had been an issue ever since I turned four or five. An underdeveloped hip joint threatened to perhaps break once I was an adult. My family strove to protect it for me.

"You have to lose weight."

"Don't run or jump, that will stress your hip joint too much."

"Don't finish that—you will be even fatter."

"I saw you jumping rope outside. Don't jump! Your hip will collapse before you are thirty years old and you will be in a wheel chair for the rest of your life."

"Don't eat those pears off that tree. Pears will get you fat, too."

"You should exercise."

"No, I don't think you should go skating again. Skating puts too much stress on your hip joint. It stresses it from the wrong angle."

"How many times do we have to tell you not to sneak food? Just don't eat so much. You'll be a cripple."

"You shouldn't have children. Being pregnant will ruin your hip and you will be a cripple for the rest of your life."

"Skiing puts too much stress your hip joint. You'll be a cripple for the rest of your life if you break it."

"Finish your soup or else you won't get anything else."

"No, no seconds. It's good to feel hungry. It gives you better dreams."

Only my mother's father refrained from telling me that I was fat and would become a cripple by the time I turned thirty. He had a dressing room, in that dressing room a wardrobe, on that wardrobe a stack of hats, and under those hats a small bag of candy. Grandpa gave me a small piece of candy to suck on once or twice a week. It was our secret.

"During the first war, we used to say in the village that the fat will become thin, and the thin will become cold to the touch," he said to soften everyone else's harangue. "And it was true during the second war, too. Here's one candy for you, and another one for your friend. Just don't let your Grandmother catch you!"

And now, the only family member who never compared my looks or intelligence to anyone else's was a whole ocean and two continents away.

I LIKED my cousin Misha a lot. She was fun and we could always talk about all kinds of things. We ended up in the same German class in school. She did a lot better—she'd been taking German in Prague, and Grandpa Stoy coached her occasionally. She seemed really shell-shocked by Princeton, though. Her English was like mine when we came a year before: given enough time she could formulate a question, but she could rarely understand the answer.

I wanted to play with her, to talk. She wanted to study. She came home from school, closeted herself in her room with the door firmly shut, and emerged for dinner several hours later. After several weeks of that, her English was pretty darn good.

"That Misha's ambitious," my mother said. "Do you see how hard she works? And she is so thin. You are smarter. I just wish you'd lose some weight. You would look so pretty."

The battle lines were drawn. I was the smart, fat one and Misha was the skinny, stupid one. Truth be told, I wasn't all that fat and she was pretty smart even though she didn't want to follow in the family tradition of becoming a chemist. From the time our mothers began comparing our attributes aloud, however, Misha became the enemy. She was an ambitious bookworm, and she was thin. And I didn't even know how it had all gone so wrong.

"Misha, want some more ice cream?" I'd ask her as I ate mine. American ice cream was like manna from heaven, plentiful, and it came in a rainbow of flavors. Not like the fake banana flavored ice cream in Prague, which was available only in the summer.

Misha wasn't interested in ice cream. We sat behind the house under a big willow tree, the winter slowly yielding its iron grip.

"I wish we had more money," Misha said.

"I babysit," I said. "Maybe you could, too."

Misha's brow furrowed, her brown eyes hooded by long, curved lashes.

"I have to watch Marketa all the time anyway," she said, referring to her younger sister. "I don't want to watch another kid, too."

Even as a three or four year old, Marketa was sent out with her older sister to play in the streets of Prague, expected to keep up with a gang of older kids. They were both given the run of the streets of Munich in the same way, while their parents made funerary wreaths to earn their stipend from the Sozial-Amt, which had apparently gotten a bit smarter as the refugees kept streaming through its doors to ravage its monetary reserves.

"We could ask our dads if they need any help," I said.

Our dads worked together in a small lab which my father rented and furnished. My father was a genius who invented awesome hydrogel polymers. My uncle was "just" a mechanic with some extra schooling, but he was also very smart and inventive. He could take things apart and put them together again, or he could take things apart and make entirely new machines out of the pieces. Give George a blender and an old TV set bought at a flea market, and he'd give back an intergalactic communication satellite, properly tuned to the Xerxon Galaxy protocol. Now he applied his gifts to making machines for the lab so they wouldn't have to be bought, and contributed his own inventive ideas about the nature and the future of hydrogel medical devices.

My father's job at the Styrofoam factory was getting worse. That was good though—as soon as his brother's family had their own apartment and the new venture capital financing came through, he could get fired. Getting fired, he was told, was better, because he would retain unemployment compensation and benefits.

"Don't get fired too soon," my mother said. "You're financing two families and a company on one salary. We have no reserves. What would we do if something happened to you?"

"THERE GOES another pan," my mother said to Aunt Vera stoically as my father and my uncle fried a hydrogel rod on a non-stick pan in a bit of oil. They grabbed the slippery sausage in two pair of pliers, and pulled, stretching it longer and thinner. Then it was tied into a stretching frame with strings.

Misha and I stood and watched. Our new job was to tie the hydrogel rods onto the frame after my father and my uncle fried them.

Uncle George bent over to inspect our work.

"This is too loose!" he said toward Misha sharply. "We are not paying the two of you a dollar an hour for something we'll have to redo ourselves later."

Misha and I tried to out-stubborn the slippery sausages, but they slipped and slid around, still slick from their cooking oil, still stretched. To stay stretched, they needed to go on the frame, and fast.

"It's really hard," I said. "I think my fingers aren't strong enough to tie the knots tight enough. And it keeps slipping."

Misha and I earned several dollars each before we were dismissed. It was our first experience in the family business.

THE ADULTS sat around the scarred kitchen table, smoking and drinking white jug wine. It was just another night of reminiscing and bonding. The smaller kids were sent off to bed after eight, but Misha and I, taking advantage of our more advanced years, got to stay for a while longer.

They told stories of other refugees who'd journeyed to Australia, only to find it socialist; the friends they missed, the government they despised. As the jug grew lighter, the mood grew heavier. Misha and I looked at one another. It was time to clear the field.

I was almost asleep when sounds of loud voices roused me. It was well after midnight. The crashing and yelling continued. Patrick woke up on the mattress by the other wall.

"What is it?" he asked.

"Oh nothing, people just got drunk. Go back to sleep."

He sat up on his bed. "I can't go to sleep," he said with the stubbornness of a five-year old. "They are too loud."

I sighed. "Let's just wait. They will get tired and go to sleep, and then we can go to sleep, too."

It didn't take long before Misha knocked on my door.

"Katka, what are they doing?" she asked, her eyes wide.

"They are drunk."

"I know they are drunk. My mom and dad get drunk too. But it sounds like they are fighting."

I heard my mother scream obscenities. Something crashed against their bedroom door with frightful force.

"Marketa's scared."

I got up and went to see Marketa, Misha right on my heels. Marketa lacked her customary cheer. Her blond hair hung limp along her face, and her eyes were red with tears.

"I don't like it," she said, trying not to sob.

"Don't worry, that's nothing, it's just people being drunk. Would you like to come to our room? We can all stay there."

And so we sat on Patrick's mattress, on the floor, covered by a comforter passed down to us by a kindly neighbor.

Our ears were straining.

We couldn't go to sleep.

There was a quiet knock on the door and Aunt Vera slipped inside like a shadow, the door closing quietly behind her.

"Here you are," she said. Her lips were smiling, but her serious eyes were searching ours. "Why aren't you asleep?"

"Mommy, I am scared," Marketa sobbed and launched herself at Aunt Vera. Aunt Vera caught her, and settled on the edge of the mattress.

"We can't sleep because of the noise," I said. "The girls can stay here until they get tired of fighting."

I liked that Aunt Vera came over. I didn't like being in charge.

"Is it my mom?" I asked after a few heartbeats.

She looked at me with that humorless smile, and nodded. "Does this happen a lot?" she asked.

"No, no, not a lot," I said, suddenly defensive of my mother. "Only once a month or so."

I saw her eyes widen.

"And it's not usually as bad as this time, either," I said.

"What do you and Patrick do?"

"We just try to ignore it. Sometimes Patrick comes to my room." I thought a bit. "This is a bad one," I acknowledged. "Usually she's asleep by now."

Aunt Vera looked at her watch. She might have been one sheet to the wind at eleven, but now it was two in the morning and she seemed entirely sober.

"You kids should be asleep," she said.

Suddenly, I felt like I had to do something. I got up and marched out of my room, Aunt Vera behind me.

"Don't go there," she said, beseeching. "You'll only make it worse."

I shook my head stubbornly.

My father's voice penetrated through the hollow-core door.

"Please stop. I am telling you to stop! Everyone can hear you!"

"I can't stand those whores!" my mother's voice yelled. "I will get those communist pigs!" Another object crashed, this time against the doorjamb right in front of me. My father called her name; she told him to screw off.

"If it wasn't for you we wouldn't be here!" she yelled. "Stuck in this asshole of a stuck-up village!"

I knocked and opened the door.

"I would appreciate it if you would be quieter. Nobody can sleep," I said in a loudly into the empty space, forcing an attitude of adult calm.

"Fucking whores! Those communist pigs even have my dog!" My mother screamed. A crashing sound, like an avalanche of sharp and fragile objects clanging against the sink, punctuated her outburst.

"Stop. Stop now. Do you want your children to see you like this?" my father said in a last-ditch effort before she rushed out of the bathroom again, fully naked, her hair long and wild, her face a painful grimace.

"Too late for that," I told my father.

He spun to face me.

"What are you doing here?" he said sternly.

"Do you realize what time it is? It's after two o'clock in the morning. Misha and Marketa came to my room, and Patrick is up too. Marketa was crying because she is scared, then Aunt Vera came in to check on us."

He looked at me with a helpless, haunted expression.

"I don't know what to do with her," he said. "Just go to your room. She will settle down."

On my way out, I glimpsed a Pert shampoo bottle on the floor, its plastic body entirely shattered, the green liquid oozing onto the cork tile floor. I wondered at the strength required to throw a bottle that hard. I was scared of the fury behind the hand that threw it. Yet this was no time for tears. No, we were never allowed to show fear. No sadness. No homesickness. Showing negative emotions wouldn't help the family with its struggle to build a new life. We had to be positive. We had to *smile*. Negative emotions had no place in our new world.

I battened down the hatches and went back to my brother and cousins.

"It's Mom again. Yep, she is drunk. But don't worry, everything will be fine in the morning."

I CAME HOME from school tired that day. Misha disappeared into her study pattern. I went to get a snack in the kitchen. Food was my friend. It was accessible, delicious, and its comfort gave me an illusion of a warm, protective blanket over my shoulders. It was always easier not to show fear, or sadness, or homesickness with so much food on hand.

My mother and my aunt sat in the kitchen, frozen in a odd sort of wary stillness. I greeted them with care, moving like a cat in a junkyard, uncertain about the fireworks that were, and the fireworks that might be.

"Your mother wants to say something to you." Aunt Vera's voice tingled like heavy, fat raindrops that broke the stillness before the storm. I suppressed a shiver and turned around to look at her. Step by step, I backed across the kitchen until my back was planted against the sink.

My mother was sitting in her usual chair. She looked pulled together now, dressed and wearing makeup. Only the dark circles under her eyes remained.

"I'd like to apologize for last night," she said with great dignity. "It seems I drank a bit more than I should have." Each word left her throat as of its own accord, unconnected to the other words that floated in a random pattern around the kitchen.

And saying this would make everything okay?

Out of nowhere, unfettered by tact or reason, words flew out of my mouth. "You got shit-faced."

My mother jumped up and faced me straight on.

"I just apologized. I expect you to accept that. And don't you dare say that again if you know what's good for you."

I gazed into her green eyes surrounded by green eye shadow and black eyeliner. Her heavy mascara weighed down her lashes. She stood there, coiled as a snake, unblinking, her mouth set tight. And at that moment, I felt free. I felt like I had absolutely nothing to lose.

"You got shit-faced," I said.

My mother slapped my face with her right hand so hard, my head turned. I evaluated the pain that seared my skin, and compared it to the pain I felt within. I smiled. The burn on my skin was nothing.

"You got shit-faced," I said again. Unflinching, my mother slapped me again, just as hard.

"You got shit-faced," I said.

"I already apologized!" My mother screamed, and lashed out with another hit.

It became a pissing contest. She was strong, but I was young. And her apology didn't make it all better. As I inhaled to declare that she got shit-faced once again, Aunt Vera moved in and extended her hand between my mother and my face.

"Katka, don't do it. There is no sense in it."

I looked at her. Her eyes pleaded, yet there was a twinkle of amusement in them. I looked at both of them.

"I am in America and I can do whatever I want. I can say whatever I want, too."

I turned around and stalked to my room where my cousin Misha sat, waiting to hear the full report.

Chapter 12

MEAT IS SO BASIC

April 12th, 1982, a different house on Deer Creek Drive, Princeton, New Jersey, USA

THE TREES WERE THICK with bud and the sun made its way through the cloud cover as we stood in our neighbor Irene's back yard. Mord and Irene's house was very much like the house we were renting just then: a one-level ranch with generously sized, single pane aluminum frame windows, a strong heating furnace, and four bedrooms. The yards throughout the neighborhood were a free-style affair with numerous trees, rhododendrons, and azaleas. Bulbs were coming out, the tips of tulips delicately bitten off by our herd of neighborhood deer.

Irene was very kind to us, eager to make friends with the new refugee family. Her friend Mrs. Kliment had called, and Irene had already donated copious spare blankets and kitchenware to our struggling household.

We stood next to her gray, wood-shingled house.

"Look, Katerina. Look, Patrick. We have rabbits. Those are rabbits." Irene's speech was slow and careful. I understood what she said.

I LOVED RABBITS, and I loved hare. They were best larded with bacon and roasted with root vegetables and spices. Then you had to pass the soft root vegetables and the meat juices through a sieve, add heavy cream, salt and pepper to taste, and you got to serve rabbit or hare with cream sauce over bread dumplings. Even at fifteen years of age I'd have known how to make this dish, provided I'd been allowed to touch the ingredients.

Grandpa Kandler, my mother's father, didn't eat rabbit. My grandmother always broke the rabbit's hip joints and reoriented its hindquarters to make it look like chicken. She disguised rabbit from my grandfather the way she always tried to hide cauliflower in the soup from my father: food was hard to come by, and it didn't pay to be choosy about it.

I never shared my grandfather's squeamishness when it came to eating rabbit, except for the time I was told, right at the dinner table, that the rabbit used to be my cousin Misha's pet. She'd fed her two rabbits long dandelion leaves and watched their little noses move frantically as they masticated with their long front teeth. When they got fat enough, her father, Uncle George, made them ready for the table and each family ate one. My cousin Misha was told she ate Fluffy as soon as she finished her last bite. Her parents were amused. I was not.

"It's the same meat you'd buy in the store," my grandmother had said with an indulgent smile. "Don't be silly. During the War there was no meat at all. Everybody ate their rabbits. Why, they aren't even real pets. The Schnobels downstairs will kill their rabbits, too."

The Schnobels had kept their rabbits in a cage under the balcony on the Eastern side of the house. I fed them long, juicy dandelion leaves through the wire openings in the cage doors. They were black and white, and looked soft, although I never got to touch one.

"Never give rabbits names," our tenant, Mr. Schnobel, had said. "Don't pet them, either. That way you don't have to worry whom you're eating."

Rabbits were good food. Not as good as horse sausage—and horse was another meat my grandfather eschewed.

"Once you ride a horse you can't eat it," he said.

"You rode a bicycle in the army," my grandmother reminded him tartly. "You kept falling off." She turned to the rest of us. "Imagine, an officer who wouldn't ride his horse."

My grandfather smiled the smile of the defeated. "I didn't have to feed my bicycle, either. And it didn't spook at things." He poked at the meat on his plate. "This is chicken, you say?" His suspicion was barely concealed in his voice.

"Sure it's chicken," my grandmother said. "Look at the way the legs are bent."

My grandfather cut off a piece and ate it. "Is that a piece of bacon in the chicken?" he asked. "Why'd you ever put bacon in a chicken? Are you sure it's not a rabbit?"

"It's a new recipe. I got it from Olga. And of course it's a chicken. Wherever would I get a rabbit? "

She surveyed my plate. Only half of my rabbit was eaten. "Eat your meat," she said. "Meat is so basic to your diet. We have meat at least three times a week in our family. We are so fortunate. There are people who can afford it only once a week. All they have is potatoes and cabbage."

THE EARLY SPRING sun tickled my nose, making me want to sneeze. I looked at my brother, feeding insipid blades of grass to Irene's black and white rabbits.

"Aren't those nice rabbits?" Irene said. Her English was slow and careful for our benefit.

I nodded with enthusiasm, searching for words. Irene beamed, waiting. My mother exuded encouragement, hoping that her first-born would express proper appreciation of the rabbits for the whole family.

"When will you kill and eat the rabbits?" I finally spat out my sentence as my brain ached over the unfamiliar syntax.

Irene straightened her thin frame as though she stepped on a live wire and her dark eyes bugged out of her narrow face, her black hair suddenly wild.

"Kill them and eat them?" She shrieked out a high-pitched, incredulous screech. "We will not kill them and eat them. They are our PETS!"

"Rabbits not pets. Rabbits very good. My mother make good rabbit sauce," I countered mildly, hoping to be the mature voice of reason my family could learn to respect. In the corner of my eye I caught the jerky, distressed movement of my mother's hands. I turned to see her wring them, searching for words of her own in a desperate frenzy.

"We not eat pets. No, no, no! We are in America now. We go to A&P and buy meat!"

Chapter 13

K-MART

May 1ˢᵗ, 1982, Deer Creek Drive, Princeton, New Jersey, USA

PRINCETON WAS a university town, and therefore we had to move a great deal. After a six-month stint on Jefferson Road, our lease was up and the owner returned from his sabbatical. He wanted his little green ranch house back, so we had to pack our meager possessions. That is, my mother packed our meager possessions, cleaned the house for the owner, and directed my father as he packed the new-to-us Toyota Celica. Three carloads later, we were unloaded into a brown ranch house further down Deer Creek Drive. My cousins' family had moved to an apartment in nearby Kingston. The new place looked fine to the rest of us, but my mother cleaned it one last time while we waited, so it was decent for us to move into.

Our rental on Deer Creek Drive had an immense living room, glazed in floor-to-ceiling windows. There was a dining room area near the walk-through kitchen end, and a smaller den right off the kitchen where my brother and I watched television after school. Everybody knows that in order to learn a new language, you need to immerse yourself. Patrick and I immersed ourselves in Scooby-Doo and Battlestar Gallactica on a regular basis, eating pan-fried Steak-umm sandwiches on Wonder Bread.

"My parents got their visas," my father announced. I tore my attention away from the braised beef, letting the brown onion sauce soak the grains of instant rice.

"When do you think they will visit?" my mother asked.

"In the spring. The airplane tickets are the cheapest then."

The news of my paternal grandparents' visit was greeted with enthusiasm, planning, and activity. Where would they sleep? What would they sleep on? What did we need to keep two more adults in relative comfort for a period of six weeks?

THE FOURTH bedroom had been intended as my father's home office. It became my parents' bedroom instead, with the desk pushed to the side and the mattresses resting on the bare floor. Grandma and grandpa got the master bedroom with the large, comfortable bed in deference to their age, and also to make their old knees and backs more comfortable.

Somebody had remarked, "I hear there are second-hand stores in Trenton where stuff is much cheaper." We mounted an expedition. Several hours later, two used, twin-size mattresses were strapped to the roof of the Toyota Celica lift-back.

The Celica was hardly a car made for moving mattresses, but in my eyes, it was a car made for moving fast. It had a sleek front and a rounded back and you could fit an amazing amount of stuff inside its cargo space.

Patrick sat behind my father, who drove. I sat behind my mother, who navigated. Patrick would lean forward between the two bucket seats.

"I see a Zero! A Zero at two o'clock!" He made a guttural airplane noise.

"Got it, captain!" my father shouted back. He grabbed the parking brake and gently vibrated it up and down, pumping the safety lock button on the tip of the lever.

"Trrrrr! Trrrrr!" The imaginary bullets hit the imaginary Japanese plane, and both of them cheered. The Zero went down in flames.

"Must you guys be playing in this traffic?" my mother asked in a tired voice. We were going as fast as the mattresses allowed.

"It's a target-rich environment!" my father replied happily. "Right, Patrick?"

"Right! Dad, I mean Captain, a Messerschmitt! A Messerschmitt coming from nine o'clock!"

We coasted to a red light. My father turned a baleful eye at a silver Cadillac, moving in from the left side.

"Let's get him! Trrrrrr! Trrrrrr!"

"Trrrrrr! Trrrrr!"

Shooting the cars that crossed our paths was the best because you got to time your gun noises just as they swooshed by. I didn't think that being fifteen meant I should miss out on all the fun. Sometimes I joined in on the shooting, too.

I LOVED shopping trips. At first, when we came to America, we would go to the supermarket every other day. We walked through the aisles in a state of serious contemplation, our shopping cart almost empty.

"Look at all those brands of instant coffee," my mother said. "It's so hard to get in Prague. Which one should we buy, you think?"

We didn't know about commercials yet, so we were pretty much on our own.

"They had Nestlé in Germany. If it was no good, they wouldn't import it," my mother decided, and a glass jar of dark coffee crystals was carefully deposited in the bottom of the shopping cart.

Every single thing was so attainable. My father's job at the Styrofoam factory was rife with unpleasant politics, but it paid a decent amount and we could afford a great deal. We felt like we should make up our mind in the most scientific, rational way on which brands to buy. The only way to do that, it seemed, was to buy, test, and compare. This resulted in an overfilled shopping cart, which would inevitably cost way too much.

"Let's return most of these things," my parents decided. And we tracked back through the almost deserted supermarket aisles, returning the redundant items, hoping to perhaps try that one brand next time for the sake of comparison. There were multiple brands of everything: bread, tea, juice, shampoo and toothpastes, even eggs.

After two or three months, we moved up to comparing supermarkets to one another. Imagine, various brands of supermarkets! And they had different prices for the same items! It was fabulous. We could figure out what was on sale where, clip enough coupons, and our scientific sampling process would become more affordable.

Much was done to avoid unnecessary expense.

"Look, they have salami and cheese for just a third of the regular price here," my mother noted. The ends of various sausage and cheese rolls were shrink-wrapped on their Styrofoam trays.

"I guess these are what's left over after the rich," my father said. He gave a wry grin, putting a good spin on buying the loaf ends. We ate the leftovers after the rich with glee. What a deal! These were perfectly good cold cuts. Maybe the Americans were too spoiled for eating the ends of a ham or a bologna roll. It was just fine by us—more for our table, and for a lot less money.

"Maybe we don't have to go to the supermarket that

often anymore," my father hazarded an opinion.

"Maybe we don't," my mother agreed. "Every time we go for two or three things, we bring two entire shopping bags. We're spending too much money."

I was disappointed. I thought the supermarket was great fun. After all, they even had make-up, and I managed to cajole my mother into buying me a bottle of nail polish.

"Don't go wild with it," she warned. "You shouldn't wear it to school, the teachers could get offended."

"Mom, the girls wear even mascara and eye shadows. A light pink nail polish is nothing." And she sighed, and put the nail polish in the cart.

WE HAD all kinds of hand-me-down clothing and bedding and kitchenware. It was donated by the friends of Mr. and Mrs. Kliment, and much appreciated. It was also very diverse, and we were ready for an upgrade.

The stores at the Quakerbridge Mall had all that we needed, but we bought nothing because it was all shockingly expensive. We went to the Quakerbridge Mall several times, because every item of merchandise in every store deserved our careful attention and scrutiny. We walked through Macy's and Sears and J.C. Penney's and all the other smaller stores, looking at everything from automobile tires to ladies' lingerie, bath towels, curtains, overcoats, shoes, plastic organizers, and even jewelry. Everything got a fair shake. In a market economy, we had to be educated customers. We were in our own cultural literacy crash course.

SpacePort was a video arcade. Once we found SpacePort, there was no going back to careful merchandise comparison as a family. My brother begged for quarters so he could play Atari and shoot down airplanes, and my father was only too happy to chaperone him. We'd developed a routine.

"Everyone synchronize your watches," my father said as we sat on the rim of the water fountain by the mall escalator.

"I am looking for three things," my mother said. "Let's meet here in one hour."

"Can we meet at McDonald's instead?" I begged.

"Yes, yes, McDonald's!" shouted Patrick.

We went our separate ways. My father took Patrick to SpacePort, where they fed quarters into fun video games. My mother and I sometimes shopped together, but I usually split off and went exploring. I was big enough already, and here in America we didn't have to worry about the Czech secret police nabbing one of the kids.

I had a few dollars from babysitting, and I had some of my lunch money saved up. That amounted to a lot, sometimes even twenty dollars. Every time I passed the water fountain by the escalator, I shot the coins in the water a wistful look. Most were just pennies, but you could see a flash of silver here and there. It would be so easy. But when Patrick and I went coin diving, people stared at us. Our parents made us stop.

"You can't do that anymore. We're in America now."

GRANDMA AND GRANDPA Stoy were my father's parents. Their arrival precipitated many more trips to stores. They had a whole list of things that were not available in a centrally planned economy. They had also always brought a little something back for every single child and grandchild in their considerable family still living in Czechoslovakia. There was much shopping to be done. But we were ready! Sure we could take them to the Quakerbridge Mall, where we would admire all those interesting items available for sale and culminate our expedition by splitting a large order of french fries at McDonald's. When it came to playing for keeps, though, nothing topped K-Mart.

Our little Toyota Celica pulled up to the front entrance of K-Mart on Route 1. My father opened his door and got out of the driver's seat. My grandfather carefully stepped out on the passenger's side. He had long legs and bad knees, and so he got the most comfortable seat in the car. My mother sat behind my father, and my grandmother behind my grandfather. The men tilted the front seats forward so the women could get out of the car. We were starting to attract attention. It's not every day you see a sporty little hatchback with four adults in it, especially when two of them are elderly. Once the women were helped out, my father came around the back and unlocked the trunk.

"Out you go! End of the line!" he said.

"I can't get out until Patrick does," I said. I was lying curled around in the trunk of the little car, enjoying the cozy curvature of the large glass window above me. When I assumed an open fetal position, there was enough space for Patrick to sit with his back against the rear seats, watching traffic from the big rear window and shooting down the Zeroes and Messerschmitts on our tail.

Patrick got out, and heads turned. It's not every day you see a kid get out of the trunk. Then I arose from my concealed position and slithered out, feeling the eyes of all those ordinary people on me. They were envious. They didn't get to ride it the trunk like I did. Our car was just like a circus clown car. The ordinary people were stuck with their ordinary sedans, and I felt sorry for them.

"This is the greatest store ever," my father told my

grandparents with a gleam of excitement in his eyes. "They have everything. Just about everything for the whole house. For the whole family!"

We stood by the front door, looking down the main aisle. The department signs were clearly visible.

"I am going to buy a drill. We need a new drill since I had to take our old one to the lab," my father said.

"And they have toys! Even battleships!" Patrick informed us from down under, vibrating with excitement. "And tanks! And planes! Can we go look at the battleships?"

The men went off to hunt for manly things, such as power tools and tools of destruction. The women headed for the clearance racks in the clothing department.

"They always have things on sale," my mother explained to my grandmother. "I always look here first."

"Look! Is that gold?" My grandmother reached out to examine a carousel loaded with earrings. They were small studs, set with genuine birthstone gems. "You can't get gold jewelry at all anymore. The girls would be so excited."

I peered at the price tags. One pair of fourteen carat gold earrings, with opals, for only $9.99. Even I could afford them.

Our unorthodox mode of transportation saved us a lot of money. You see, if you fill the whole car with people, including even the trunk, you really can't buy all that much and take it home with you. Each shopping trip was more like a reconnaissance mission. We saw the treasures of gold earrings, exquisite and paintable battleship models, clothes, power tools, new stereos, and the pretty porcelain china set with a thin gold band around the rims. But since we couldn't transport it all, we had to go home first, empty the people out, and make a return trip. That gave us time to think more carefully about the purchases, and often to rethink them entirely.

"I wouldn't shop at K-Mart," Mrs. Kliment said in a voice borne of firm conviction. She paused delicately. "You have to be so careful about their quality."

"The tools are the same brands as in other stores," my father argued. "And they cost less. They are all placed together. You can pick whatever you want."

"True," she said, and paused for a moment as she tugged on the hem of her elegant woolen sweater from Landau's at Nassau Street. She looked down at her manicured hands, as if to make sure that her gold jewelry still radiated an understated gleam of prosperity. Then she leaned over, as if to tell a secret. "Blacks shop in K-Mart a lot," she said. "We get blacks coming all the way from Trenton to shop there."

"You don't shop there because blacks from Trenton shop there?" I asked. The logic escaped me.

My mother turned her face toward me, her features stern. 'That was inappropriate,' her expression told me, but her eyes twinkled with glee. She enjoyed seeing Mrs. Kliment back-pedal. If K-mart merchandise was good enough for us, it was good enough for anybody.

Chapter 14

BOYS WILL BE BOYS

August 5th, 1982, Deer Creek Drive, Princeton, NJ, USA

Every culture has its rites of passage. Boys know how they stepped over that threshold from boyhood to manhood. In the old country, they would become men during the two years of compulsory military service. Here in the US, they'd get a summer job and a girlfriend, start to shave every day, and maybe get laid if they played their cards right. The transition was slower and less defined, its edges lacking in crispness. Some boys stayed boys forever.

How did girls become women, exactly? Not through marriage or childbirth. Not through sex. Competence wasn't a highlighted characteristic of womanhood in either culture. Back in the old country, I would have begun ballroom dance lessons at the age of fifteen, which would lead to dating, high heels, and an extended curfew. At fifteen, I'd have gotten my national ID and would have been considered an adult in the eyes of the society. People would expect me to dress better, behave calmer, and be considerate and dignified. They would address me by my last name instead of my first, since I'd no longer be a kid.

After years of sucking up to people older than myself and using honorifics when addressing them, I couldn't wait. I was going to become Miss Stoy. Nobody would dare use my first name unless they knew me well enough. Even the teachers would address me formally.

Except we were in America when I turned fifteen, and the magical transition just failed to happen. Everybody acted the same, and I don't think I've ever felt more cheated in my entire life.

When I turned sixteen I got my learner's permit. Getting a driver's license was, in many respects, much like getting a national identification card. That summer, I drove around Princeton, my father in the passenger seat, his face grim and his hands clenched on the seat.

His right foot kept slamming the carpeted wheel-well as he tried to brake before I did, as he tried to go through the intersection a bit faster than I felt comfortable.

He taught me to parallel-park, to stay in my lane, to always use turn signals, to buckle up before I even turned the engine on.

I got my driver's license that year, and I felt more independent, but the transition from girlhood to womanhood hadn't—quite—occurred. I worked in the lab and babysat, earning good money, but when I was thirteen in Germany I earned money fishing out coins out of water fountains, so even that wasn't all that special. Earning money is what people do, not what adults do.

Maybe I should go have sex, I thought, but there was nobody special I had in mind. The callow football team assholes wouldn't spare me a look, and the fun geeks in my science classes didn't know how to hit on a girl.

Adulthood eluded me.

THE SUMMER I got my drivers' license was so hot that the asphalt shimmered under the relentless New Jersey sun. Almost every Saturday, my mother packed up lunches and drinks and snacks and towels, my father shoved them in the car along with suitable reading material, Patrick added his sand toys, and we headed for the beach.

Two hours of dense traffic fumes later, we focused on finding a strip of sand and parking where the beach was free of charge and where we didn't rub shoulder to shoulder with the hordes of Puerto Ricans and blacks. We had nothing against them in particular, but it was a given fact that Puerto Ricans and blacks were poor.

We didn't want to hang out with the poor. We wanted to hang out with the rich. My parents chose not to pay five dollars for the beach, but it was easier to pretend we weren't poor if at least half of our neighbors were white.

Racist? Not remotely. Moneyist? Definitely.

We baked in the sun, slathering sunscreen on our backs and hoping it wouldn't wash off in the waves. We bodysurfed and looked for shells and observed the odd, fossil-like horseshoe crabs while the brazen seagulls tried to get into any food that wasn't secured in my mother's zippered beach bag. We never bothered with a cooler – they looked like such a pain to drag across the dunes, and besides, coolers were expensive.

By the time two o'clock passed we tired of the waves and settled down with our books. My seven-year old brother, Patrick, sat in the sand, his body covered with tan streaks from unevenly applied sunscreen. He didn't read much, not back in second grade. Czech and English still mixed on his tongue when he did his homework, and his intellectual interests were inclined toward a better understanding of the in-flight maneuverability differences between various World War II airplanes. He filled our world with Japanese Zeroes, German Messerschmitts, Wildcats and Hellcats, Flying Fortresses and

B-52 bombers. His second-grade mind strove to engulf the whole corpus of historical military knowledge—the statistics, combat performance, size and number of guns, casualties. He lived and breathed airplanes and battleships and aircraft carriers, with an occasional dinosaur or volcano tossed in for good measure.

No wonder, then, that his sand fortress looked a lot like Tobruk or Gallipoli with its smooth, sandy walls punctuated with openings for cannons, and with entrenchments of sticks and strings that imitated the deadly field of combat.

My father, an inveterate history buff, was his greatest accomplice. They discussed weapons and strategies and generals; their triumphs as well as their defeats. Away from work at last, my father had enough time to give his young son his undivided attention. His large, gifted hands sculpted realistic battlements. His inventive streak used old yogurt cups to dig foxholes for machine guns. Patrick ran down the beach, collecting plastic bottle caps for land mines, and my father joined him in his search.

There was no lack of found art objects at the beach that year. This was the summer of the Garbage Dispute. The states of New York and New Jersey were engaged in a petty territorial dispute over who got to dump garbage where and for how much.

The situation peaked as barges, full of municipal garbage, sailed up and down the coast in search of harbor privileges and a friendly landfill. They were denied access at every turn. The news showed the stinky heaps of garbage bags that fell off the boats, bobbing on the waves like misshapen buoys. Some of that garbage got washed ashore, but the beaches were never closed. We turned our noses up at the pollution and ignored it. Under regular circumstances, my father would exhort us to pick up wrappers after other people and throw them out at home. He was the first one to bend his back and stoop for some unknown slob's empty soda can.

This time he just let it lie.

There was just too much. So much plastic, it embedded itself into one's emotional landscape, the vision of bottle caps and sun-bleached yogurt containers burned into the back of our retinas, along with the relentless, crashing waves, the slow-moving horseshoe crabs, and the rude and noisy seagulls.

My mother put her book down. "I better go cool down some. The sun's hotter than it looks, even with the breeze." She rose out of her folding chair and stumbled down the hot, uneven sand to the water's edge. I watched her regain her footing on the firm, wet sand, going in just knee deep, past the last breakers, and splashing her shoulders to ease in. It looked so good. I realized how hot I was and reached for the insulated bottle of iced tea.

"Here, come look at our fortress! It's so realistic!" My father waved at her as she emerged from the shallow waves, and she angled toward them, curious.

I WATCHED her facial expression change from one of polite attention to hissing disapproval. My mother was mad over a sand fortress. Now *that* was interesting. I put my book down and walked over.

"How could you," I heard her sputter in her low-pitched Czech. "That's just unspeakable."

My father saw my shadow approach and lifted his gaze to me, eyes crinkled in amusement.

"Look! Your brother and I made an entire Mediterranean fortress. Here are the outer defenses… the mine field… the anti-tank trenches…. isn't it great?" I nodded.

It was, actually, quite impressive and my younger brother was beside himself with glee.

My mother's sharp tongue cut it. "People are looking at it again."

"Let them look. We put a lot of work into it." He looked at me, expecting admiration. "Look! The fortress is even armed with anti-aircraft guns!"

I nodded, leaning closer to inspect the sun-bleached plastic tubes. I recoiled.

"Dad!"

"What?" All innocence.

"Dad, do you know what those are?"

"What?" Amusement, now.

"Those are plastic tampon applicators!"

"Yeah. Your mother already informed me."

"But that's unsanitary!" I wailed in Czech. People kept passing us. The men and their boys were inspecting the grand fortress with proper appreciation, the girls with indifference, their mothers with a mixture of disgust and pity.

The pity was directed, by and large, at my irate mother and at me. Regardless of any language differences, the topic of disagreement was out in the open, brazenly displayed for all to see.

"It's not unsanitary," my father replied, employing his voice of scientifically-justified reason. "Don't you know that salt water kills germs? Well, so does the sun. UV irradiation is a well accepted germ-control method. These were here for weeks, if not months. I bet they are cleaner than our hands."

"This is bullshit," my mother exploded. "Some black woman in Harlem put these you-know-where, and now weeks later, you and your seven year old son are here, touching them!"

I absorbed her words, and internally rejected them. There was something wrong with what she'd said, but I wasn't sure yet where the sense of wrongness came from, and I didn't feel brave enough for an argument. The tampon applicators were, beyond a shadow of a doubt, disgusting.

My father looked at me for support. I had none.

"But look! They even have a built-in recoil mechanism!" He reached over to the nearest anti-aircraft gun, moving its outer, formerly pink barrel forward and back. He looked at me again, beseeching, hoping I would see the beauty and the logic of it all.

"Real cannons have a mechanism just like this. It's important, especially on board ships; otherwise, the force of the blast would push them back." He looked at the tampon applicator with new eyes.

"Do we still have those blueberries? That might be just the right size for ammunition."

"I'll get them!" Patrick jumped to his feet, happy that his father wouldn't yield to unreasonable, illogical pressure and wouldn't abandon his precious anti-aircraft guns.

I met my father's eyes with solemn regret. "Dad, this is really gross. It might be clean and sterilized, but… other women, strangers, *used* these." I didn't have it in me to get more graphic than that. "They… they *used* these, and then they threw them out. They have cooties now."

My mother and I leveled him with a cold, disapproving glare. We turned our backs on him and went in the cool water, and it was at that point, I think, that I became a woman. I sided with the clean and the sensible, the proper and the decent. A girl, now a *girl* might be persuaded as to the virtue of used, sun-bleached, ocean-washed plastic tampon applicators as anti-aircraft guns.

A *woman*, not so much.

Chapter 15

HOW IS THE DOG?

August 20th, 1983, Robert Road, Princeton, NJ, USA

"So how's the dog?"

We asked that question often in our numerous letters to Grandma and Grandpa.

"Can we bring her here?" I asked wistfully.

"We are working on it. I have to find out more about how it's done," my father said.

"We'd need to rent a house with a fenced yard," my mother said. I felt a slight undercurrent of an objection in her statement.

"Mom, you don't want Karina to come here?" I asked, flashing her a challenging stare.

She sighed. "I miss her, too. But it's not as simple as you think. Look at these American dogs. They're such wimps. She'd have them for breakfast."

I looked out the window. Two owners walked their pooches on leashes. The dogs were so mild—they simply ignored one another. They ignored other pedestrians, as though they didn't have a single territorial bone in their bodies. Compared to our dogs, these American dogs appeared downright sedated. My mind wandered back in time to Karina, to her soft fur and her intelligent eyes.

When I'd been ten years old and my baby brother Patrik sat on our mother's lap in the kitchen, my father stood before her as though on trial. He held a fuzzy furball in his arms.

"I can't believe you'd do a thing like this," my mother said. "You could have at least called!"

"You are right, I should have called. But don't you think the children would like to see the puppy, just for a week or so?" My father had the voice of honey and his eyes were pleading, excited.

"May I have a look?" I asked.

"See, the kids are curious. This is very educational." My father bent over and let me see the brown fuzzball in the crook of his leather jacket. I saw two sleepy eyes, and a big pink tongue that searched for my finger. I took her in my arms and smiled. Her German Shepherd ears pointed to the sides as though drunk, tipped with dark brown fur, and she smelled good.

My mother watched me examine the puppy and her angry eyes softened somewhat.

"I want the dog out of the house by the time the week is over," she said.

"We'll have to find her a home," my father said meekly. "I am sure lots of people would love to even buy her. She has such excellent lineage." He bent over the pup and stroked her between the ears with his finger.

"So how did this happen, anyway?" my mother asked, feeling that momentum had shifted against her for the moment.

"One of the experimental dogs we are testing hip replacements on, she got pregnant and had two puppies. She is an excellent bitch, retired from the border guard. But there wasn't any money allocated for puppies in the research budget, so they were going to kill them." My father's voice hissed with outrage. "Imagine, killing dogs like that. What a waste! The mother is a dog of legend. So my coworker and I, we gave the handlers a bottle of rum each, and they were glad to give us the puppies." He took a deep breath. "That's why I can't take her back."

My mother thought it was a waste, too, but suggested somebody else could have taken the pup in.

"I just wanted to show her to the children. This is no ordinary dog. This is one quarter wolf."

My mother straightened and shot a baleful glare at my father. "You brought a wolf-dog into a house with children?"

Patrik wiggled on her lap, eager to see what I had.

"Her mom is a half wolf, with an impressive service record. They are wonderful with families. Why, the border guard interbreeds their stock with wolves on purpose, just to keep their senses keener." He took the puppy from my hands and presented her to my mother and to Patrik.

Patrik said, "Guuoo! Gagagaga!" and launched himself toward the dog, his hand touching her soft fur. She looked up amiably, and my mother made first eye contact with her. From that point I knew the odds were good that we were going to have a dog. Not just any dog, a wolf dog. My mother named her Karina.

WOLF DOGS don't housebreak as easily as more domesticated breeds, and Karina's runny feces stained the white kitchen linoleum forever. Every weekday morning, my mother was the first one to bravely enter the kitchen and wash the floor. Every weekend morning we would all hold our pee, pretending to be asleep, hoping that somebody else would get up first and take care of it all.

"Take the dog out," my mother told me. "Make sure she does something outside, then praise her." Then she went to change Patrik's cotton diapers.

Karina took over the small balcony, rendering it useless for humans. And she grew and grew. Dad trained her in basic obedience and when she was ready, I was allowed to walk her. In fact, for almost four years I took her on long walks well outside my permitted area, secure in the knowledge that nobody would lay a hand on me. Karina was protective of her people, and nobody sane would mess with a forty-kilo, overprotective wolf dog. When Patrik had learned to walk and ran down the sidewalk in that odd, free-fall gait of toddlers, Karina trotted between him and the street. She learned to do her business outside, and my father brought men from work to build her a fenced-in run and a doghouse.

ONE WINTRY Sunday, we returned home from our afternoon walk. My mother was making hot chocolate to go with the *buchty* pastries my grandmother baked on the weekends. Patrik was on the floor next to Karina, playing.

"I have a colleague doing some research at the Prague Zoo," my father remarked casually over a cup of hot chocolate. "Apparently their puma female gave birth to too many little mountain lions. They'll have to kill most of them." He sipped the foam off the hot chocolate and added a splash of rum.

"Don't even think about it," my mother said, her voice as hard as a railroad track.

"I could just bring a cub for the children to play with, then I can take it back."

"Oh, Mom, please!" I said, my eyes ablaze with adventure. "Mom, please, please can we get a mountain lion?"

Most of my schoolmates begged for a goldfish, or a kitten, or at most, a puppy. The absurdity of my request brought a twinkle of humor to my mother's eye.

"You apparently have no idea what a mountain lion eats," my mother said.

"It's not like feeding the dog, where I have to cook rice every day, save all table scraps, and buy extra meat to mix it in. Pumas want high quality, red meat. Our family has meat at least three times a week, and I consider that a success."

I hung my head. I knew about the meat shortages. I knew about the kilos of chicken necks, cooked for soup, where the meat had to be laboriously picked off for the dog. I knew of the disgusting bovine udders, floating bloated in the stockpot, being made into dog food so cheap even Karina turned her nose at them.

"I guess you're right. No puma would want to eat cow udders," I said sadly. Yet that night I dreamt of walking down the street among my school friends and school archenemies, a supple, muscular puma on one leash, a loyal, intelligent wolf dog on the other.

"I GOT A LETTER from Grandma," my mother told us over dinner. "We need to send her one hundred and twenty dollars for the dog cage."

My father recoiled in his chair. "So much? It's just a dog cage!"

"They aren't available like you see them here. They had to custom-build one from scratch."

"And there's no way to get around the quarantine period in England?" my father asked.

"No—all flights from Prague to America go through London. She'd have to be quarantined for two months in a kennel. It's their law over there." My mother frowned.

Two months in a kennel was a long time, especially for a wolf dog.

"Mother wrote that she still goes nuts when those Arab students walk by," my mother remarked. "She barks at the Vietnamese, too."

"And here we have those too, plus a lot of blacks," my father said.

"How can she tell?" I wondered.

"Even people can tell. Your grandfather's best friend fought with the RAF in the Second World War. He had a black friend there. They teased one another about smelling different. If people can tell, so can dogs. Especially a wolf."

Karina stayed in Prague. It was the best way. She didn't have to suffer transport, and my grandparents got to enjoy her pleasant company for years. She even attacked a policeman who'd entered the house without a warrant. The multicultural community of Princeton could rest at ease, undisturbed by a politically incorrect, Eastern European wolf dog.

Chapter 16

ONLY IN AMERICA

October 3rd, 1983, Princeton High School, Princeton, NJ, USA

I WAS A JUNIOR at Princeton High School and a boy was interested in me. He was about my height, his hair was brown and his features unremarkable, but he was interested in me and that made him downright fascinating. We stood in a tiled, institutional high school corridor, waiting for the cafeteria doors to open.

"Hi, I'm Ryan," he said, not quite meeting my eyes. He smiled a little. His shoulders were bunched up around his ears and he kept swaying from one foot to another. He wore brown sneakers and jeans and a red button-down shirt.

"I'm Katerina," I said. I waited to see what he would do. A boy who talked to me was a curiosity, and I was interested to see how he would act.

"Are you hungry?" he asked. I shrugged. That was actually a loaded question. Saying "yes" would have meant I was going to eat, and eating was a physiological function. One didn't do such things in front of a boy. Saying "no" would be stupid—why else would I be waiting for the cafeteria to open?

Minutes later, we were let in and I bought my customary chocolate chip cookies and skim milk. I sat down at an empty table, bent over a biology textbook, when a shadow fell over my page. I looked up and there he was, brown hair and red shirt, shoulders bunched up even higher, and still swaying from side to side.

"Can I sit here?"

I nodded silently, because my mouth was full of the dry, cheap chocolate chip cookie. After three years in the country, I could go through the day without the safety blanket of my large dictionary. Conversation was still a bit halting, but Ryan didn't seem to mind.

I decided to adopt Ryan as a temporary boyfriend. Not because of some undying love or irresistible attraction – only because other girls had boyfriends, and I was curious to see what it was like to have one.

People saw us walk down the halls, and some would say, "Hi, Ryan!", and they seemed happy to see me by his side. None of them knew my name.

"How are you, Ryan?" an older boy asked.

"I am doing great, thanks to Our Lord Jesus Christ who saved me," said Ryan in an everyday voice. "This here is Katerina. She's from Czechoslovakia."

I nodded hello and beamed at Ryan proudly. *Just look at that,* I thought. As far as I was concerned, Ryan forged through life while exercising his First Amendment rights of free speech. He was allowed to have a religion, right in the open where anyone could hear him. He was allowed to do that, and to talk about it. Anyone was allowed to do that, and they weren't going to end up in an insane asylum or be kicked out of school or anything. This was America! We were in America and we could do whatever we wanted.

The older boy gave me a funny look and walked away. Ryan looked at me expectantly. I ambled on to my class.

"Hey," he said, catching up to me. "Wait up. What I said, did that bother you?"

I thought for a second. "Why should it bother me? You're allowed to say things like that. This is America. You can say whatever you want." My conviction in his freedom of speech was firm, and he smiled with relief.

"WHY DO YOU go out with that guy?" asked my friend Sabrina. "He's weird. The way he throws Jesus and stuff around all the time. I can't stand it."

"Well I don't believe in Jesus either, but this is America. He's allowed to say whatever he wants."

"Why does he keep saying it to us, though," she said. "I am so sick of hearing it."

We sat in a half-circle window alcove good five feet above the staircase landing. There were two staircases like that. I loved climbing up into the alcove and studying by the light that filtered through old glass panes, leaded together in an old-fashioned way and filling the neo-gothic window arches. I looked outside. There was a picnic table under a tree on the front lawn of the building, a bunch of kids sitting on it, cutting class and trying to hide their cigarettes. The small, diamond-shaped glass panes undulated with ancient glass flow, distorting the view, refracting the crystalline autumn light.

"When we were in West Germany, waiting for our American visas, we lived in the American barracks for a while," I said, watching the golden sunlight tint the pale green color of the leaves with incipient autumn cheer. "There was a church right across the street, and every Sunday, these Germans would go in, and after two hours they came out again."

"They were going to church, sure," Sabrina said, aloof. "People here do it, too."

"I'd never seen people do it before. In Czechoslovakia, my grandmother taught me two Czech prayers when I was really little. Then she told me never to tell anyone, and never to say them where people could hear me. Only at bedtime. She said if somebody knew she was teaching me prayers, my father could lose his job. Or maybe I couldn't go to a good school when I was older. I'd have to work in a factory instead."

I ripped my gaze away from the mesmerizing vitreous world and faced my friend. Her pale blue eyes widened and her freckled nose wrinkled in a scowl.

"That's so unfair!" she exclaimed. "Would they really do that?"

"I don't know," I admitted. "But we thought they might. That was enough. Anyway, here in America you can be whatever religion you want. And you can tell people, and they can't stop you. It says so in the First Amendment."

"Do you have a religion?" Sabrina asked curiously. She leaned forward, making her pale blond hair fall into her face. Anticipation tensed every inch of her lanky body.

"Sure. I am a Zen Buddhist."

Her eyes widened with disbelief.

"How could you be a Buddhist? Buddhists come from Asia."

"Aha!" I pointed a finger in the air. "But this is America. I am in America and I can do whatever I want."

"No you can't."

"Sure I can, and so can you. I went to the library and took out a book on every world religion. I like Buddhism the best, and of Buddhism I like Zen the best."

"Why?"

"I don't know," I shrugged. "It just feels right."

Sabrina leaned back against the old sandstone wall. She rubbed the length of her nose with her finger absently as she looked at me, not really seeing me.

"Oh. Okay then. But you be careful with this guy. I've heard stories that he used to run with a really wild crowd, and got in trouble."

"Ryan, with a wild crowd? No way." I leaned forward a bit. "What kind of trouble?"

She hesitated. "People talked about drugs. And he didn't come to school at all last year."

RYAN AND I walked around the school, mesmerized and self-absorbed. Hormonally insane, too. We found an outside alcove with a recessed door that hid us from prying eyes, and kissed.

The kiss wasn't what I'd thought it would feel like, but it wasn't bad, and I wanted to try some more. Kissing was fun.

"Are you a virgin?" Ryan asked suddenly.

"What is a virgin?" I asked, groping for a meaning of the word.

His face flushed up to the roots of his brown hair. "It's a pure person," he said.

I shrugged. "I am pure," I said. After all, for the last year I showered every day. In Prague we had bathed only on Sundays. How much purer can one get?

"No, not like that..." he seemed at loss for words. "It's... a virgin is a person who has never had sex. Did you have sex?"

"I don't know. How do you have sex?"

Ryan exhaled deeply and threw his head back, his eyes rolling up to the heavens in silent supplication. "I guess you're a virgin, then."

The fact that I was a virgin made him happy.

"Are you a virgin, Ryan?" I asked, rolling the new word on my tongue.

He hesitated.

"Well, sort of," he said. "I did a lot of things before Our Lord Jesus Christ saved me, but I never got to home base." He looked at my confused expression.

"I never had sex, so I am a virgin too."

My free period was almost over. I walked around the school with my first, real, American boyfriend. A thrill of adventure ran down my spine.

"Two virgins!" he said after a long pause, with his face beaming. "We are two virgins, together! And we can stay virgins together! Our Lord Jesus Christ who saved me looks down on us and smiles."

A CARTOON cross-section of an erect penis pulsated on the screen in front of the classroom. The kids howled with laughter. Even Mrs. Brown had a smile on her face. After a few seconds the scene shifted to little sperm shooting up the urethra and swimming upstream, into the cross-section of the uterus.

I felt cheated. I felt like I was supposed to be learning something, yet the supposedly graphic Health Education movie only told me what the Czech female health books described in very few words. They said "sexual intercourse" in both languages, but I still didn't know how it was done. I knew how the sperm made its way up the Fallopian tubes, I saw it fertilize the ovum, and get implanted in the uterine wall. But how did it get in there to begin with?

My mother was pleased that I'd seen the movie. "Now you know, then," she said. "So I don't have to tell you."

"But Mom, you are supposed to tell me about the Facts of Life, remember?"

My mother smiled a Mona Lisa smile. She was off the hook—I'd been exposed to enough material in school.

"All I will tell you, some women are catchier than others," she said.

"Catchier?" I asked, stumbling over an unfamiliar Czech word.

"Catchier. Some catch faster than others, so be careful around boys."

"Why? What do they catch?" I saw my mother turn out of the kitchen, going down to her and father's bedroom.

"Mom, what do you mean by 'catchier'?" I howled after her.

She stuck her head out the door. "Just remember, it takes only once." The door was shut and the conversation about my fertility was over.

RYAN AND I were at his house, his mother still at work. He showed me around. There was an oversized, red Bible on a round table in the breakfast nook.

"This is where I read the Scripture every day," Ryan said. "Our Lord Jesus Christ keeps me from temptation."

Another word I didn't know. My large dictionary was at home and my small one was in my school locker.

"What is temptation?" I asked.

"Temptation is… here, let's read the Bible together." Ryan put his hand on my arm to lead me to his Bible lair.

I wiggled out. The ancient red book was foreboding. It reminded me of those large, red-bound texts on Marxism-Leninism. It made me think of control.

I walked back to the living room with a strange sense of upset in my belly.

Control.

People telling you how to feel and what to think. Marx. Lenin. Our Lord Jesus Christ Who Saved Ryan.

"Wait, wait, don't be mad," Ryan caught up with me. We sat on the sofa, me sulking, Ryan running his hand over my shoulder in an attempt to improve my mood. We kissed, and then we kissed some more until we ended up in a semi-horizontal position. Ryan wiggled against me from behind. He moved against my hip in a rhythm that suddenly reminded me of that health class movie. Unbidden, an image of a cross-section of a cartoon, pulsating penis sprang to my mind. Right then, Ryan exuded a heavy, raspy sigh, and stopped moving.

A silent minute went by.

"Did you have fun?" he asked.

"Fun? Fun doing what?" I said, alarmed. Was something supposed to have happened?

"Fun what we were doing," he said.

"But we didn't do anything," I retorted.

"We did," he said accusingly.

"Maybe you did, but I want to have fun too,"

Ryan's eyes filled with terror. He stood up shakily, then made a motion with his hands as though he was washing them.

"I'll be right back," he said weakly and headed off to the bathroom.

Damn, I thought. Something did go on right there, something having to do with the Facts of Life. I knew it did, and I missed it! I entirely missed the whole thing! And he was too chicken to do it again.

Two days later, Ryan's lips met mine briefly before he pulled away.

"I can't kiss you," he said.

"Why not?" I asked.

"When I kiss you, I feel like I am cheating on Our Lord Jesus Christ who saved me." Misery and relief mingled in his voice.

"I don't want to have a boyfriend like that," I said.

He looked up in alarm.

"Why not?"

"Because you don't want to do anything. Because you feel like you are cheating on Christ. You love Christ more than you love me."

He didn't say yes or no. We were quiet for a while, standing under a bare tree. The cold November wind was whipping around us, chasing dry and shriveled leaves.

"My priest said to ask if you thought about my offer to take you to Church on Sunday," Ryan said.

"Did you tell him what I said last time?"

"Yes," Ryan said. "He said that a Church is where God is. It doesn't have to be a beautiful cathedral, like you had in Europe." Lack of baroque architecture had been my latest objection against meeting his priest.

"But if a Church is where God is, can't you love God anywhere? In the forest, even?" I said, seeing a loophole in the argument.

Ryan looked like a man drowning and I stifled every bit of pity I felt for him at that moment.

"We need the priest to tell us what to do," he said.

"I left Czechoslovakia because I don't want other people to tell me what to do, or what to think, or how to feel. And you're trying to do that, and you're trying to get me to your church so your priest can do that."

"Are you saying the Church is like the communist government?" Ryan asked, aghast.

"Yes. But I am in America now, and I can do whatever I want. You can, too."

I turned around and left him standing there in the cold, unwilling to play second fiddle to an unknown deity. Unwilling to have us be virgins together.

Chapter 17

A FINELY HONED BLADE

March 7ᵗʰ, 1982, Princeton High School, Princeton, NJ, USA

WHEN MY FAMILY came to America in 1980, we knew we could never return back home. Communist Czechoslovakia did not view defectors kindly. Our bridges were burned and our rose glasses firmly attached to the bridges of our frozen noses as we deplaned at JFK in New York.

We were going to become Americans—and not just any ordinary Americans, either. We would become the most red-blooded, genuine Americans the world had ever seen. And to do that, we had to learn whole new skill sets. Not just the language of the land—learning good English was just the beginning. We'd eat hamburgers and fries and drink Coca-Cola. We'd wear bathing suits while going swimming, even my little brother. We'd observe all the things our neighbors did and try to emulate their way of life. We had already learned about Thanksgiving and learned to eat strange foods, even though peanut butter and jelly sandwiches were disgusting.

There were occasions, however, when glimpses of our neighbor's lives provided inadequate instruction, and in those cases we turned to literary examples. We studied Steinbeck, Hemingway, and London. We contemplated Fennimore Cooper. We carefully chose literary archetypes and emulated them whenever possible. A real American ought to have a gun, but we couldn't do that yet because we were new in the country. A real American carried a knife. A real American was an optimistic, autonomous vision of self-reliance and capability.

My parents were on board with the plan, as evidenced by the fact that my father gave me a lovely, folding Bowie knife for Christmas. "That's so the blacks at school don't bother you," he said with a smile that might have spelled innocent mischief, but which gave me an excellent idea. An armed society is a polite society—or so I'd read—and maybe I really could stop getting bullied in school after Christmas.

SCHOOL WAS still tough going. Back in ninth grade I'd had to rely on a large Czech-English, English-Czech dictionary. My linguistic deficit put me in the slow classes. Princeton High School had a ten percent black population, but most of these students were concentrated in my classes—the slow classes. I was the only white person there. I looked different, I spoke funny, and my grades were better than anyone else's because I actually bothered to turn in my homework.

"Look at Katerina! From Czechoslovakia. She turned in her homework without even speaking English, so you all don't have any excuse!" Mrs. Brown was one of three teachers of African ancestry in the school. Holding me up as an example for the rest of the class didn't make me any friends.

There was a group of boys that always hung out in the halls, and they thought it entertaining to give me an occasional shakedown. My locker would get tossed, I'd get slammed against the metal doors, and my backpack would be ransacked for valuables. The problem persisted even once I'd earned my way out of the slow classes and into the mainstream student body. I considered complaining, but telling on a fellow student was an ancient taboo. I was in America now. And as a hard-boiled, Hemingwayesque American, I had to handle the problem by myself.

We were lined up in the hallway, waiting to enter the Auditorium. The boys who often bothered me were lined up opposite of me, and they talked and stared, their bodies vibrating with trapped kinetic energy. I leaned against the wall of lockers, pulled my finely honed blade out of my pocket, clicked it open, and proceeded to clean my nails. One by one, with great deliberation, I removed specks of grime and with great satisfaction I felt the wall of bodies across from me settle some and grow a bit quiet. They stared, they whispered. I examined my manicure and put my knife away. Despite the occasional verbal taunt, the physical abuse stopped.

ONE YEAR passed as I kept hiding behind tough attitude in the hallways and worked hard in the classroom. My knife was always in my pocket. Our gym teacher wanted us to jog across the field outside, yet I hung back. Would my knife would slip out of the shallow pocket of my sweats? There was no time to take it to my locker.

"Mrs. Jones, would you please hold this for me until after class?" I asked, extending the folded knife in my hand.

Mrs. Jones' eyes widened in her brown face. "Where did you find this?"

"It's mine. I don't want to lose it in the grass."

"Yours?" She was incredulous, her pitch higher with alarm. "You brought this to school?"

I didn't understand the cause of her distress. "Yes, ma'am. I always carry this knife with me. My father gave it to me. For Christmas."

"I want you to report to the principal's office after school. We will discuss this then."

I saw her slip my knife into her pants pocket.

"You won't lose it?" I fretted. "You are wearing sweats too!"

"I won't lose it," she sighed. "Now go and jog."

MR. VAUGHN looked at me, and through me, and said in his reasonable, quiet voice, "Now tell me, young lady, why you brought a knife to school."

It occurred to me that I could, perhaps, tell him about those black boys who keep harassing me, except Mrs. Jones was leaning her butt against the radiator few feet to my right and nailing the black kids in her hearing felt like accusing Mrs. Jones of being mean, too.

Besides, both Mrs. Jones and Mr. Vaughn were teachers. Back in my school in Prague, all the kids had presented a united front to teachers and parents alike. Squealing on students, even enemy students, felt wrong.

Un-American.

The Old Man hadn't complained about the fish being too strong or the sun too hot, and a gold-panner on the Klondike didn't complain about the cold. They made do for themselves. I sat in silence, just like them.

"Why don't you tell me who is bothering you," Mr. Vaughn said. I hesitated.

"I cannot! You are the teachers. I can't get other students in trouble."

Mr. Vaughn and Mrs. Jones exchanged a look confirming a previously reached conclusion.

"You are in America now. You can trust others. This is not like Czechoslovakia, where the police would come."

I could feel myself waver. I would have told, had it only been Mr. Vaughn. But Mrs. Jones was there, and she was black, and her feelings were sure to be hurt if I said anything bad about people of her color.

"What do the boys look like?" she asked. "Are they black?"

Defeated and relieved both, I nodded. The cat was out of the bag, and to say "no" would be to lie. In America we don't lie, or cheat, or accept bribes.

Mr. Vaughn sighed. "That group of boys who hang out in the hallways. They cause many problems. Why didn't you come for help?"

"I didn't want to cause trouble. I just scared them off with my knife, just showing it as I cleaned my nails. I wouldn't have used it to hurt anyone."

"How come a girl your age has a knife?" Mr. Vaughn said.

"All Americans have knives."

"I don't have a knife," they both said in unison as I stood there, dumbfounded. My vision of America wavered before my eyes, and something tight and heavy shook loose just then. That heavy, solid anchor of independence and self-reliance no longer dragged quite so heavy in my wake.

AS THOUGH the kids knew that I'd promised to leave my knife at home, one week later my locker got tossed and my calculator got stolen. I needed that calculator—my accelerated chemistry class was demanding and I could afford neither the time to do the calculations by hand, nor the money to buy a new one. I strode into Mr. Vaughn's office, ready to deliver my bad news and curious to see how he would, in turn, deliver on his promise. Fifteen minutes later, Mr. Vaughn gave me my calculator back. "I can't tell you who took it. That's part of the deal."

My view of a true American was under revision. The whole concept of adults helping a student was amazing. Was it American to ask for help? What were the rules on that, exactly? But I'd asked for help only within the framework of keeping a previously granted set of mutual promises. Keeping those promises worked, and it worked on both sides. Mr. Vaughn helped with the calculator, and Mrs. Jones kept near me in gym to make sure the boys didn't brain me with a basketball from behind. As that old anchor of absolute autonomy began to shed some more of its previous mass, I was surprised to find that I could stand straighter, and hold my shoulders up just a bit easier. It was just heavy enough to keep my feet firmly rooted to the ground.

THE BOYS grew taller and calmer in the course of the next year, and nobody would mess with the foreign kid who was under Mrs. Jones's protection. I grew taller too, and my expanded social circle took me to a school dance. There was a band in the gym and the lights were lowered, boys and girls either dancing disco or huddling around the bleachers.

A Haitian girl from my TOEFL-English class brought her cousin. Would I like to dance with him, she asked. He didn't know anyone. Sure, I said. I took his hand, dark against mine even in the dim light of the gym. I forget his name, but he was a good dancer. His English was worse than mine, but we meshed well together, moving to the beat of songs both fast and slow. The last slow dance of the night was being played and as my dance partner slowly turned me around, I realized we had an audience. People, all people, even teachers, were watching us. I thrilled with all that attention and limelight—dance was my secret passion and it was good to be recognized for good timing, good sense of movement. But why the interest in the slow parts?

The lights came on. I let my dance partner kiss my cheek, and returned the chaste gesture as the band started to pack their instruments. It was time to head home. As I reached the gym double door, a familiar group of black boys barred my path.

"Hey," they said.

"Hi." I was poised, ready for trouble.

"Why did you dance with that guy?" their leader said.

"He's Nicole's cousin."

"But he's black!"

I bristled. There was a charge in the air I did not understand.

"So?" I retorted. "You're black too! And besides, it doesn't matter what color you are. In America, everyone's equal."

We stood there in a pool of hermetically sealed stillness, seeing one another as though for the very first time. The smallest of the boys stepped forward, and instead of his usual cutting remark, he said, "Thank you." And he stuck his hand out. I shook it awkwardly, taken aback. Falling back on formal, European manners carried me through.

"Yeah, thank you." "Thank you." "Thank you." I shook all of their hands.

"I don't understand why you're thanking me. I didn't do anything." My words felt weak.

It took years and years before I became American enough to understand.

About the Author:

Kate Pavelle was born Kateřina Stoyová in Prague, Czechoslovak Socialist Republic. She learned to use a gas mask in first grade. She fired her first VZ50 in her sixth grade civil defense class. Her first dog was a wolf hybrid stolen from the Czechoslovak border guard, and her eccentric father blew out the windows of their house with a stun grenade. On purpose. Unlike his chemical explosions—those were always by accident.

Kate Pavelle's high-stakes, high-adrenaline childhood leaves her searching for the next exciting thing. Martial arts and travel and rock climbing. Horses and cookies and toxic mushrooms. Medieval combat and children and brain-tanning deer hide in the driveway.

Her quest resonates through her suspense, thrillers and romances, matched only by her drive to share the fun with her readers. Kate once knew the hunger of being a political refugee and the terror of being pursued by government agents. She imbues her characters with her own struggle for survival, excellence, and world domination.

Only the dead bodies are imaginary.

More by Kate Pavelle:

From Mugen Press:
    Fire and Water
    Relativistic Phenomena
    The Price of Silence

Coming in 2015:
    In the Shadow of the Red Star (Cancelled Czech Files)
    Critical Timing (a thriller)
    Amerika (Cancelled Czech Files)

Published by Mugen Press at www.mugenpress.com and available through all major venues.

From Dreamspinner Press:
    Wild Horses
    Zipper Fall
    Broken Gait
    Breakfall (Book 1 of Fall trilogy)

Coming soon:

Swordfall (Book 2 of Fall trilogy)

Published by Dreamspinner Press at www.dreamspinnerpress.com, and available through all major venues.

Sneak peek exclusive!

The *CANCELLED CZECH FILES* are vast and plentiful. Enjoy this excerpt from *IN THE SHADOW OF THE RED STAR,"* a *Cancelled Czech Files* story collection. Learn more about my misspent youth behind the Iron Curtain.

FIRST MEMORIES
August, 1968, Prague, Czechoslovakia.

The rim of the green plastic potty was digging into my butt. My mother, father, and grandmother huddled around the radio that sat on the kitchen table under the window. The big window was closed despite the heat—only the small, lift-up window in the sloped ceiling let a trickle of fresh air in—but I was too focused on the adults to care.
"Wheeeeeeee-wheeeeeeee-wheeeeee!"
"Dammit they're jamming the station again. Vlada, try a different frequency!" My grandmother recognized my father as the fixer of all things mechanical. My father obliged. An excited voice came out of the box once again, but it was the wrong kind of excited.
"They have tanks in the Wenceslas Square," my grandmother said, and I knew what a tank looked like, because my father drew it for me once along with cars and dogs and airplanes.
"Wheeeeee-wheeeeeeeee-wheeeeee-wheeeeeee-wheeeeee!" The screech coming out of the radio was downright hypnotic.
"She should go to sleep," my mother said, but there wasn't much resolve behind her statement. Lately, when the grownups sat around the radio, I got to stay up too, mostly because my little bed was in the kitchen. My father

lit up a cigarette and inhaled. The acrid odor of the spent sulfur match mingled with the familiar smell of tobacco smoke. My mother pulled one out as well, fumbling with nervous hands.

"Light me up," she said, and my father leaned over. She touched the ends of their cigarettes together and made the tips glow. Then she leaned back and let the smoke out of her mouth in a dainty stream. I liked the way it swirled in the air, growing thinner and thinner, until it finally dissipated in the stuffy kitchen air. A droplet of sweat ran down my nose and to my lip. I licked it. It was salty, like buggers.

"Jaja, don't smoke!" my grandmother told my mother.

"Katka, don't pick your nose!" my mother told me.

"Oh, dammit. Here, gimme that. Those godforsaken Russkies!" My grandmother took my mother's cigarette out of her mouth and pulled on it, hard, making the tip bright orange. We all had something in our mouth that didn't belong there. I dug a finger up my nose once again just as my grandmother began to cough.

A loud, sharp crack split the air.

The light went out.

A shower of hot glass covered my arms, my hair.

The silence stretched, punctuated by a few lone crackles on the radio.

I began to cry.

"Somebody shot out the light!" That was my grandmother's voice. It was dark already, but my little eyes began to adjust and I quieted down and looked around.

"Don't move," my mother said. She was so close, I could feel her breath in my hair. She touched my arms with careful, light fingertips. "She's covered in glass!" When I heard the alarm in her voice, I began to cry again.

"There's that sniper across the hill," my father said.

"He must have shot the light out through the roof window."

The hushed, grownup discussion was drowned out by the alarmed voice on the radio and the Wheeeee-wheeeeee-wheeeee sound of the radio jammer.

My father turned on a little light in the cooking alcove of the kitchen. "This has a red lampshade and a small bulb. It shouldn't be visible from across the hill," he said. "Let's get the glass off her first."

Coming out in 2015, and available whereever fine books are sold.

www.ingramcontent.com/pod-product-compliance
Lightning Source LLC
Chambersburg PA
CBHW071501040426
42444CB00008B/1438